Buried in Georgetown

A Brief Look at Cemeteries and Burial Grounds in Georgetown, Washington, D.C.

By Peter T. Higgins

Buried in Georgetown

Copyright © 2022 by Peter T. Higgins
All rights reserved.
No portion of this book may be reproduced, by any process or technique, without the express written consent of the author.

The Publisher is not responsible for third-party websites or their content. All URL links were active at time of publication.

All photographs used in this book were taken by the Author unless otherwise noted. All photographs taken by the Author remain the property of the Author and may not be used without the express written consent of the author.

Buried in Georgetown
An Historical Review
Includes bibliographical references and appendixes.

ISBN 978-1-7351238-6-8
Tender Fire Books
www.TenderFireBooks.com

Printed in the United States of America

Visit us on the Internet at
https://higgins-dc.com/books/

Table of Contents

Introduction 1
   Vocabulary of burial places 1
   The organization of this book 2
   My background and motivation for this book 3
Georgetown Cemeteries by Categories 4
Georgetown Cemetery Histories Alphabetically 10
   Female Union Band (FUB) Society Graveyard 10
   Interestingly, a similarly named Society still exists in Georgetown 11
   Georgetown Lutheran Cemetery 13
   Georgetown University Jesuit Community Cemetery 16
   Holy Trinity Parish Cemeteries 20
      Holy Trinity Graveyard 21
      The Old College Burial Ground (also Known as Holy Trinity Cemetery #2) 23
      Holy Rood Cemetery 26
   The Methodist Cemetery 30
   Mount Zion Cemetery 31
      The Old Methodist Episcopal Burying Ground 32
      The Female Union Band Society Graveyard 33
   Oak Hill Cemetery 38

- Presbyterian Church Cemeteries 42
  - The Bridge Street Presbyterian Graveyard 42
  - The Presbyterian Burial Ground 44
- Visitation Community Cemeteries 53
  - Visitation Burial Crypt 54
  - Visitation Community Cemetery (The Garden Cemetery) 58
  - Visitation New Cemetery 59
- Yarrow Mamout Private Burial Site 62

Bibliography 69

Researchers of Note 71

Acknowledgments 73

Appendix A: Orientation to Georgetown of 1796 75

Appendix B: A Brief History of Georgetown 1632 – 1899 78
- Georgetown, the early days 78
- 1740s 79
- 1750s 79
- 1760s 79
- 1770s 79
- 1780s 80
- Georgetown in the early days of The District Of Columbia 81
- 1790s 81
- 1800s 82
- 1810s 83
- 1820s 83
- 1830s 84
- 1840s 84
- 1850s 84
- Georgetown – Emancipation And the Civil War 84
- 1860s 84
- 1870s 85

Georgetown – at the end of the 19th Century 85
1890s 85
End Notes 88

Table of Figures

Figure 1 – Map of Georgetown with all Cemeteries Numbered 8
Figure 2 – Picture of the Old Woman's Home (The Lutz House) 13
Figure 3 – The Jesuit Community Cemetery in Snow 17
Figure 4 – Tombstone of First Burial in the Jesuit Community Cemetery 18
Figure 5 – Location of Jesuit Cemetery 19
Figure 6 – Signage on West Side of the Jesuit Cemetery 20
Figure 7 – Map of Holy Trinity Cemetery #2 & Visitation New Cemetery 24
Figure 8 – Location of Holy Rood Cemetery on an 1874 Map 27
Figure 9 – Holy Rood Cemetery Sign 28
Figure 10 – The Columbarium Construction Report from the Dedication 30
Figure 11 – Picture of Holy Rood Columbarium Granite Wall 30
Figure 12 – Mt. Zion Cemetery / FUB Cemetery History Plaque 32
Figure 13 – Mt Zion & FUB Cemetery Picture 34
Figure 14 – Plat of Mt. Zion Cemetery 35
Figure 15 – Willow Columbarium at Oak Hill 40
Figure 16 – Renwick Chapel at Oak Hill 41
Figure 17 – Humorous Burial Marker 42
Figure 18 – Location of the Presbyterian Church & Graveyard on Bridge Street 43
Figure 19 – 1887 Map of Georgetown with Several Sites Marked 51
Figure 20 – 1887 Map of Presbyterian Burial Ground and Chapel 51
Figure 21 – Visitation Campus Map with Burial Areas Marked 54
Figure 22 – Visitation Crypt 55
Figure 23 – Visitation Garden Cemetery in 1890 59
Figure 24 – Visitation New Cemetery in 2020 60
Figure 25 – Details of a Tombstone - Visitation New Cemetery 61

Figure 26 – Entrance to the Visitation New Cemetery 61
Figure 27 – Peale's 1819 Portrait of Yarrow Mamout 64
Figure 28 – Photograph of Yarrow Mamout Archaeological Dig 68
Figure 29 – 1796 Map of Georgetown 75
Figure 30 – Forest Marbury House History Plaque 82
Figure 31 – 1899 Map of Georgetown with Lyons Mill Road Marked 87

Dedicated to my fellow members of the Holy Trinity History Committee who have helped me learn about Georgetown History – the good and the bad.

Alpert, Peter
Butler, Marilyn
Cook, Bernard
Flanagan, Brian
George, John
Hentges, Harriet
Klick, Ashley
Nystrom, Linda
Maco, Paul
Moran, Mary
Noonan, Suzanne
Nystrom, Duane
Nystrom, Linda
Simonson, Nancee

Introduction

In 2013 I started researching for a planned history book, <u>God Lives in Georgetown, A Brief Look at His Many Houses</u>. In my research for that book, I came across numerous references to cemeteries, graveyards, and burial grounds. While there are only a handful still in use in Georgetown, I found that over time there have been several others, ranging in size and in their affiliation with a church, family, or group of people. Later I decided to split the research material into two books by moving all the material on cemeteries into this separate book – which I then have worked on, as time permitted, since the summer of 2020, setting aside the church history book for a while.

Vocabulary of burial places

It is important to note that burials were traditionally on church grounds, typically known as graveyards. Over time, many Georgetown church graveyards (e.g., Georgetown Lutheran Church's graveyard) were moved or covered over. As graveyards filled up, more space was needed and land separate from the church property was acquired and set aside for burials. These burial places were known as Burial Grounds or Cemeteries, depending on the organizers of the sites.

When speaking of places where deceased persons' remains or their cremains have been interred, I often use the more generic *cemeteries.* When discussing specific cemeteries, if the place has a formal name and type of burial place such as *Burial Ground*, then I use that name and type.

Peter T. Higgins

In the past few years two of Georgetown's cemeteries each added a columbarium for the entombment of cremains: Oak Hill Cemetery and Holy Rood Cemetery.

The organization of this book

The rest of this book is organized as follows:

- Maps showing the location of the cemeteries over time as well as the changes of the Georgetown boundaries and streets – interspersed, as appropriate, throughout the book.
- Tables of cemeteries in Georgetown, classified as still operating, merged / moved, or closed to include the date established. They are then numbered and marked on a current map of Georgetown.

    - From the 18th century through the early 20th century there have been several Family Cemeteries in Georgetown – I have chosen to not address them, as little is known. I recommend Paul Sluby's <u>Bury Me Deep</u> (see Bibliography, page 69) for those interested in Family Cemeteries, as he has researched all of them.
    - I followed with great interest the 2015 excavation associated with the Yarrow Mamout Private Burial Site and there is a section about Yarrow Mamout's life and death included among the Georgetown Cemetery histories. It is a story worth reading all by itself. Mamout's burial site is an exception to the *no-family cemeteries in this book* rule.

- Georgetown Cemetery histories – organized alphabetically, with pictures and maps, as appropriate.
- Bibliography
- Researchers of Note
- Acknowledgements
- Appendices (additional historical facts for readers interested in deeper exploration into the history of Georgetown)
- Endnotes

My background and motivation for this book

I moved to Georgetown in the summer of 1968 and lived on P Street just west of Wisconsin Avenue, diagonally across from the Savile Book Shop. Back in 1851 that would have been on 5th Street just west of High Street. My two housemates, then serving in the US Army, went to Viet Nam a couple of months after I moved in. The rent was more than I could afford for a single occupant – so I moved to the suburbs of Northern Virginia, where I worked. They returned safely from their time in Viet Nam and we are still in touch and friends 50 some years later.

In 1970 I married Kathleen M., from back home in New Jersey, and we moved into The Commons Apartments in McLean, VA, near Tyson's Corner. By 1972 we moved into the city and lived in Glover Park and we were members of Georgetown's Holy Trinity Church – which I had joined back in 1968. Fifty years later I still live in the city and enjoy walking to and around Georgetown.

In April 2016 my wife, Kathy, succumbed to cancer and at that point the parish cemetery, Holy Rood, was not accepting burials but plans were under development to add a columbarium to the cemetery. The columbarium was dedicated on November 2, 2019. On June 6, 2020 – our 50th Wedding Anniversary, Kathy's cremains were interred at Holy Rood's new columbarium, one of the first dozen or so internments.

When I started researching this book I did not plan on or even think about our family ending up in one of the cemeteries in this book. Since I purchased a double niche in the columbarium, I know where my cremains will be – with Kathy's forever.

Georgetown Cemeteries by Categories

Buried in Georgetown

The tables below list the cemeteries by classification, they are then described in alphabetical order to make searching easier on the reader. All addresses are in Georgetown, unless otherwise noted.

1. Cemeteries still active in Georgetown (i.e., people are still being buried and / or cremains are still being entombed)
2. Major Georgetown Cemeteries closed and completely gone
3. Georgetown Cemeteries now inactive and in major disrepair
4. Cemeteries of significant interest on private property in Georgetown

In the case of many family cemeteries – over time, the remains were reinterred in another cemetery and the family cemetery, on the property with the residence, is simply gone.

Table 1 Georgetown Cemeteries Still Active

Name	Date Established	Current Address
Georgetown University Jesuit Cemetery	1808	Georgetown University Main Campus
Georgetown Visitation Monastery Cemeteries	1821	1500 35th Street NW
Holy Trinity Church's Holy Rood Cemetery	1832	2126 Wisconsin Ave. NW
Oak Hill Cemetery	1849	30th and R Streets NW

Table 2 Major Georgetown Cemeteries Closed and Completely Gone

Name	Date Established	Comments
Georgetown Lutheran Church Graveyard	1769	Formerly on the property surrounding the Lutheran Church at 1556 Wisconsin Ave. NW.

Holy Trinity Church's Cemeteries prior to Holy Rood	1794	The two locations pre-dating Holy Rood have been closed and removed.
Presbyterian Church Cemeteries	1802	Original Bridge Street Graveyard closed in the 1820s and the Presbyterian Burial Ground closed in 1908 – now the Volta Park Recreation Center.

Table 3 Georgetown Inactive Cemeteries In Major Disrepair

Name	Date Established	Current Location
Old Methodist Episcopal Burying Ground	1808	Now part of the Mount Zion Cemetery Complex
Female Union Band Society Cemetery	1842	Now part of the Mount Zion Cemetery Complex
Mt. Zion (Methodist ME Church) Cemetery	1879	Lyons Mill Road, and Mill Road, Georgetown – see Figure 31

Table 4 Cemeteries of Significant Interest on Private Property

Name	Date Established	Previous Location
Yarrow Mamout Private Burial Spot	N/A	3324 Dent Place NW

There were at least 7 family burial plots / graveyards in Georgetown – none of them are existent today in the sense that they are visible and clearly marked. They are described in Sluby's book but not in this book except for one. The most famous of these private burial sites is the Yarrow Mamout private burial site at 3324 Dent Place (called 6th Street in 1847, S Street by 1887, and now Dent Place as of 1915). The details about The Yarrow Mamout site are provided below with the other cemetery histories, in alphabetical order.

Buried in Georgetown

To make the cemetery locations easy to find, I have marked-up a map (Figure 1) of Georgetown with the unique reference numbers as listed in Table 5. The Map is from the DC Government web site and shows Advisory Neighborhood Commission (ANC) #2 – Georgetown. The Blue symbol and the address 1627 33RD Street should be ignored, they come with the map.

Table 5 List Of Cemetery Numbers for Figure 2 Map

No.	Name of cemetery	Alternate names
1	Georgetown Lutheran Church Graveyard	
2	Georgetown University Jesuit Cemetery	
3	Georgetown Visitation Monastery Crypt	
4	Georgetown Visitation Monastery Garden Cemetery	
5	Georgetown Visitation Monastery New Cemetery	
6	Holy Trinity Church Graveyard	
7	Holy Trinity Cemetery 2	The College Ground
8	Holy Trinity Holy Rood	Trinity Upper Graveyard
9	Presbyterian Bridge Street Graveyard	
10	Presbyterian Burial Ground	
11	Oak Hill Cemetery	
12	Old Methodist Episcopal Burying Grounds	Mt. Zion Cemetery
13	Female Union Band Society Cemetery	FUB Cemetery
14	Mt. Zion Methodist ME Church Cemetery	Mt. Zion Cemetery
15	Yarrow Mamout Private Burial Spot	

Figure 1 – Map of Georgetown with all Cemeteries Numbered

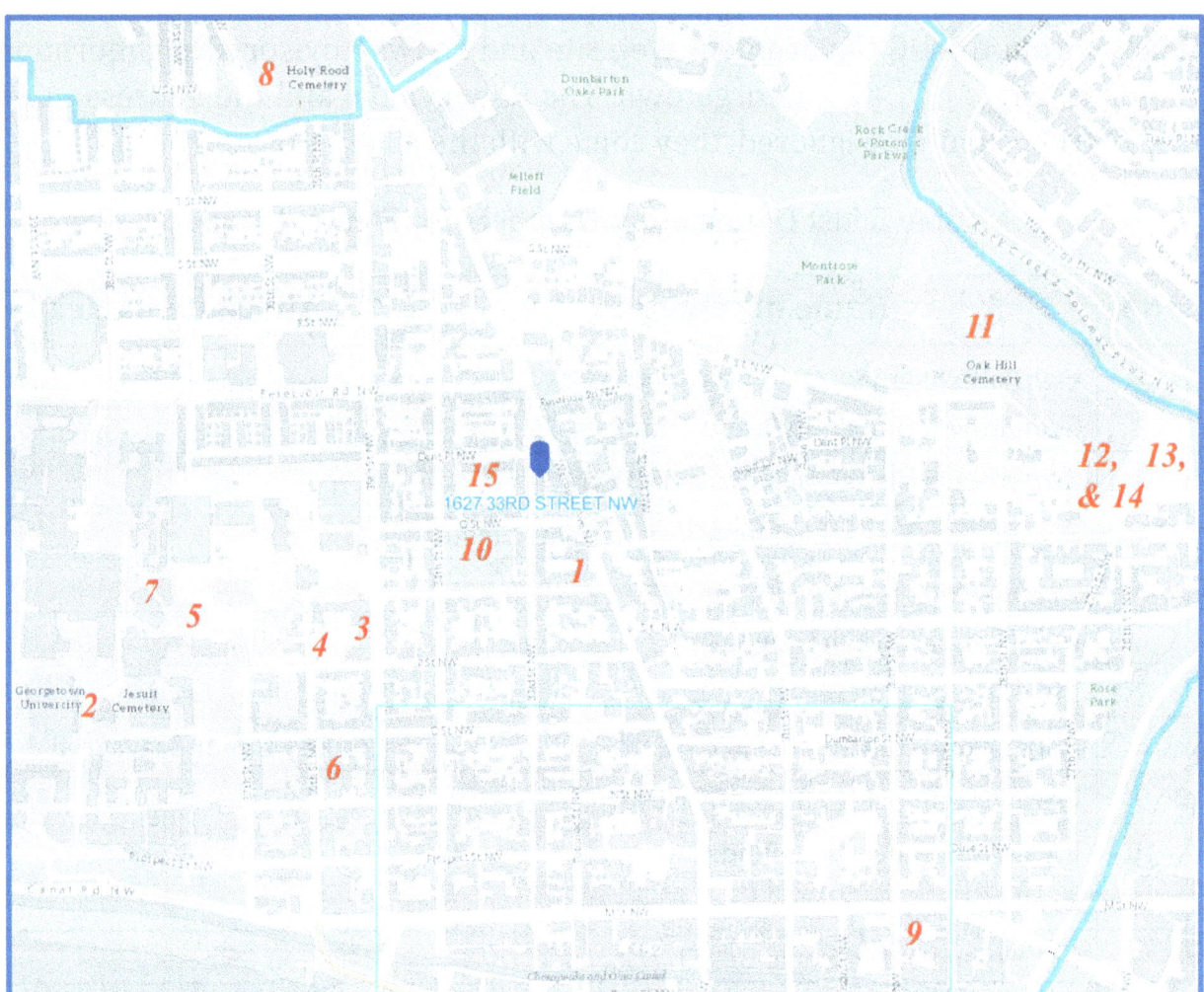

An interesting aspect of the number of cemeteries over time (excluding Yarrow Mamout and other family cemeteries) is that out of the 15 listed above – only 4 are still operational:

2. Georgetown Jesuit Cemetery

8. Holy Rood Cemetery

11. Oak Hill Cemetery

5. Visitation New Cemetery

The other 11 have ceased operations and in most cases are long gone. In some cases, there are no records of where the remains were removed to or even if they were removed – paper records destroyed in fires or simply unavailable. An example is the Georgetown Lutheran Graveyard – the very one protected by the Supreme Court decision – no records are known to exist as to where the remains might have been moved to when the current church was built. There are at least three cases where subsequent construction has unearthed remains – they are discussed in the appropriate sections of the next section. Two of them involve Holy Trinity cemeteries and one involves the Presbyterian Burial Grounds.

Georgetown Cemetery Histories Alphabetically

Female Union Band (FUB) Society Graveyard

In 1842 the Female Union Band Society, a cooperative benevolent society of free Black women whose members were pledged to assist one another in sickness and in death, was created and they purchased the land for the Female Union Band Society Graveyard.

Given the laws and policies of the time, the Society had to hire a man to purchase the land for them – likely it had to be a White man. We see in the Historic American Landscape Survey DC-15, Mount Zion Cemetery/ Female Union Band Cemetery (Old Methodist Burying Ground):

> *On October 19, 1842, Joseph E. Whithall of New Orleans sold a tract of land along the western border of the Old Methodist Burying Ground for the "sum of $250 current money." Joseph Mason purchased the land "in trust for the coloured Female society called the Female Union Band Society of the County of Washington in the District of Columbia."*

The land was off Mill Road and Lyons Mill Road in the Herring Hill neighborhood of Georgetown. Over time the society dissolved and the cemetery fell into disrepair. The grounds were adjacent to the Old Methodist Episcopal Burying Ground, which also fell into disrepair.

In 1879 both of these cemeteries were taken over by the Mount Zion United Methodist Church at 1334 29th Street; the church dates back to 1809. The joint cemeteries are believed to have been stops on the Underground Railroad.[i] Today they are often referred to simply as the Mt. Zion Cemetery. See the Mt. Zion Cemetery entry in this book for more details.

Interestingly, a similarly named society still exists in Georgetown

An 1877 map of Georgetown shows a Female Union Benevolent Society owning a house on Wisconsin Avenue where the Aged Woman's Home is now located, at 1255 Wisconsin Avenue. The Aged Woman's Home of Georgetown was formerly known as the Female Union Benevolent Society of Georgetown.

It appears that the similarity of the names of the two *Female Union ... Societies* is a quirk of incorporating a charitable group and the two Societies appear to have nothing further in common other than, of course, Georgetown's women. The information is included here for the enjoyment of the readers and to distinguish the two Societies, in case others come across this similarity and arrive at the wrong conclusions.

In 1867 the organization "The Female Union Benevolent Society" was formed in order to provide refuge to women stranded in Washington and Georgetown after the Civil War. Their web site provides a brief history:

> *Following the end of the Civil War, many women were widowed and in dire financial straits. In late 1867, "The Female Union Benevolent Society of Georgetown" rented what is now one of the oldest houses still standing in Georgetown [The Lutz House] to house some of these women. The Female Union begged door-to-door for funds to maintain the house. In February of 1868, Mark Twain gave a lecture at Forrest Hall in Georgetown on the Sandwich Islands (Hawaiian Islands) for the benefit of the Female Union. ... The name was changed in later years to "The Aged Woman's Home of Georgetown" (the Home) and has been in continuous operation since the start. The mission is to provide a safe and affordable shelter for women who are*

> *at least 62 years of age, in good physical and mental health, and whose finances do not exceed the poverty level. The Home can accommodate 11 women.[ii]*

The Benevolent Society rented the Lutz House and eventually purchased it outright. The Lutz house is famous in its own right as John Lutz, a Revolutionary war veteran who served as George Washington's bodyguard at Valley Forge, opened a business there starting in 1804 as well as living there. The Benevolent Society purchased it on June 20, 1914.[iii] They had rented the house continuously since February of 1868 – 46 years!

The Figure 2 is a photograph of the Aged Woman's Home of Georgetown; note the significant number of steps up to the house – a Home for Aged Women! It is on the east side of Wisconsin Avenue between Prospect and N Streets.

Figure 2 – Picture of the Old Woman's Home (The Lutz House)

Georgetown Lutheran Cemetery

The church website provides a brief history of the church and graveyard. Some portions of the website are provided below:

> *Thirty-two years before the city of Washington became the capital of our nation, a Lutheran congregation was organized in Georgetown, north of the Potomac River. A deed recorded in Frederick, Maryland, May 17, 1770, and a decision of the Supreme Court in 1829 concerning the title to a Lutheran church property prove the*

> *existence of an organized Lutheran congregation in Georgetown as early as 1769.*
>
> *Early in the 18th century, a group of Lutherans from Germany, having settled in Pennsylvania, Delaware, and Maryland, migrated to the Potomac Valley. They were attracted by Lord Baltimore's offer of land. Itinerant pastors ministered to these settlers as early as 1733. A generous pioneer developer donated a plot for the erection of a Lutheran church and a congregation was promptly organized.* [iv]

The property included room for a burying ground and it was used in the late 1700s. The web site GLC250.org (short for *Georgetown Lutheran Church 250th Anniversary* – one presumes) has some history notes added in October 2019 that relate to the burial grounds and landmark legal case. The notes are provided here as the legal case established an important precedent for ownership of burial grounds. A parish history booklet notes that when the log church became dilapidated, ownership of the property was challenged in 1824. The details are available on the parish website: GLC250.org and in a 2019 history of the first 250 years.[v]

> *By the early nineteenth century, Georgetown Lutheran Church was in disarray. The original log cabin church built in 1769 had fallen into disrepair, and regular services were no longer held.*
>
> *There remained, however, a burying ground on the land that had been allocated to the Lutheran Church by Charles Beatty and George Frazier Hawkins in 1769. Grave markers for early members of the congregation were clearly visible, and the land had been fenced to keep animals away.*
>
> *The heirs of Beatty and Hawkins saw in the derelict church building an opportunity to reclaim the land deeded to Georgetown Lutheran Church and use it to develop new, more lucrative, buildings. According to court documents, they entered the property and "threw down the fence and tombstones." Georgetown had grown considerably since 1769, and was now more densely populated, with rowhouses sharing space on the streets with businesses and public buildings, ...*

Although the church building had fallen down, there still existed a voluntary society of Lutherans, and they filed an injunction seeking to end the trespassing and resolve the dispute over the land title. The case eventually found its way to the U.S. Supreme Court, where it is recorded as Beatty v. Kurtz, 27 U.S. 566 (1829).

The heirs of Beatty and Hawkins claimed that the 1769 deed to the Lutheran church was conditional, which would have terminated the title when the church fell down and was not replaced.

The Court found in favor of the Lutherans. Justice Joseph Story, writing the unanimous opinion of the Court, affirmed a perpetual injunction against the heirs of Beatty and Hawkins (the defendants).

Here is a key extract from the decision:

"This is not the case of a mere private trespass; but a public nuisance, going to the irreparable injury of the Georgetown congregation of Lutherans. The property consecrated to their use by a perpetual servitude or easement, is to be taken from them; the sepulchres [sic] of the dead are to be violated; the feelings of religion, and the sentiment of natural affection of the kindred and friends of the deceased are to be wounded; and the memorials erected by piety or love, to the memory of the good, are to be removed so as to leave no trace of the last home of their ancestry to those who may visit the spot in future generations. It cannot be that such acts are to be redressed by the ordinary process of law. The remedy must be sought, if at all, in the protecting power of a court of chancery; operating by its injunction to preserve the repose of the ashes of the dead, and the religious sensibilities of the living."

The Beatty v. Kurtz decision is considered a foundation of U.S. law regarding cemeteries and the status of human remains for several reasons.

- *It emphasizes the importance and special status of burying grounds.*

> - *It places burying grounds under the protection of a public court in the absence of an established church or ecclesiastical courts.*
> - *By referencing "irreparable injury," it signals that the appropriate remedy to the "public nuisance" caused by the intrusion is equitable relief, not money damages.*

The Beatty v. Kurtz decision spurred a renewed energy in the Lutheran congregation, and a second sanctuary was built around 1835. The cemetery remained undisturbed until the construction of a parsonage on the land in 1920, which likely caused the graves to be removed.

If the bodies were reinterred in a different cemetery, the church did not keep a record of it. The author reached out to a number of local cemeteries, who could not locate a record of re-burials from our site in 1920-21, and were unable to provide any additional information as to the current resting place of the earliest members of the congregation. [vi]

Georgetown University Jesuit Community Cemetery

In 1808 the Georgetown College (now University) Jesuit (Society of Jesus) Community established the Jesuit Community Cemetery on the college campus. However, this site is not its original location. The Jesuit cemetery was laid out in its present location, north of the Old North Building, in June 1854. The 1808 cemetery was actually established close to what is now the southern end of Healy Hall. The first burial, of Thomas Kelly, N.S.J., occurred on August 16th, 1808. Forty-six Jesuits were buried in the original cemetery before it was moved north to its location today. The change came because Maguire Hall was being constructed in 1854 to house students of the prep division and university administrators did not want the new building to be adjacent to the cemetery.[vii]

Figure 3, below, shows the cemetery in early March 2015 after a snowstorm. This is a peaceful scene in the center of the hustle of university life.

Figure 3 – The Jesuit Community Cemetery in Snow

Figure 4, picture of the Kelly headstone, is included here and it appears to be a relatively new replacement as many of the tombstones from the early years are no longer as readable. It is possible that it was replaced when the original forty-six Jesuit graves from 1808 were moved to the current location but it appears even newer than that time period. Note that Thomas Kelly died in his novitiate year (N.S.J.) – about 10 months after joining the Jesuit community. As in other Jesuit cemeteries I have visited, many of the headstones list the date of birth (Natus, in Latin), the date the person entered the Jesuits (Ingressus), and the date of death (Obit).

Figure 4 – Tombstone of First Burial in the Jesuit Community Cemetery

Among the noteworthy people buried in the Georgetown Jesuit Cemetery is the Rev. Patrick Francis Healy who was a Religious Leader and Educator; he was the son of an Irish immigrant, Michael Healy, and a former slave, Mary Eliza Healy.

Patrick Healy became the first Black in America to earn a doctorate degree. He joined the Jesuits and ultimately became the 29th president of Georgetown University, serving between 1873 and 1882. As such, he was also the first Black to serve as president of a predominately White American university.[viii] One of the main campus buildings is named after the Rev. Patrick Healy.

The cemetery is open around the clock as are all of the open areas of the campus. There is a simple sign urging visitors to show respect and not to walk on the actual graves. The initial 1808 graves are behind the evergreen tree in the left of Figure 3. The University has detailed records of the burials in this

Buried in Georgetown

cemetery, which can be accessed in the Levinger Library – special collections division.

Figure 5 shows the location of the Jesuit cemetery relative to the Healy and Copley Halls and the Georgetown University main campus entrance at 37th and O Streets. The cemetery is marked and labeled on the satellite image.

Figure 6 incorrectly states that these tombs have been here starting in 1808; it is true that they have been on the Campus since 1808.

Figure 5 – Location of Jesuit Cemetery

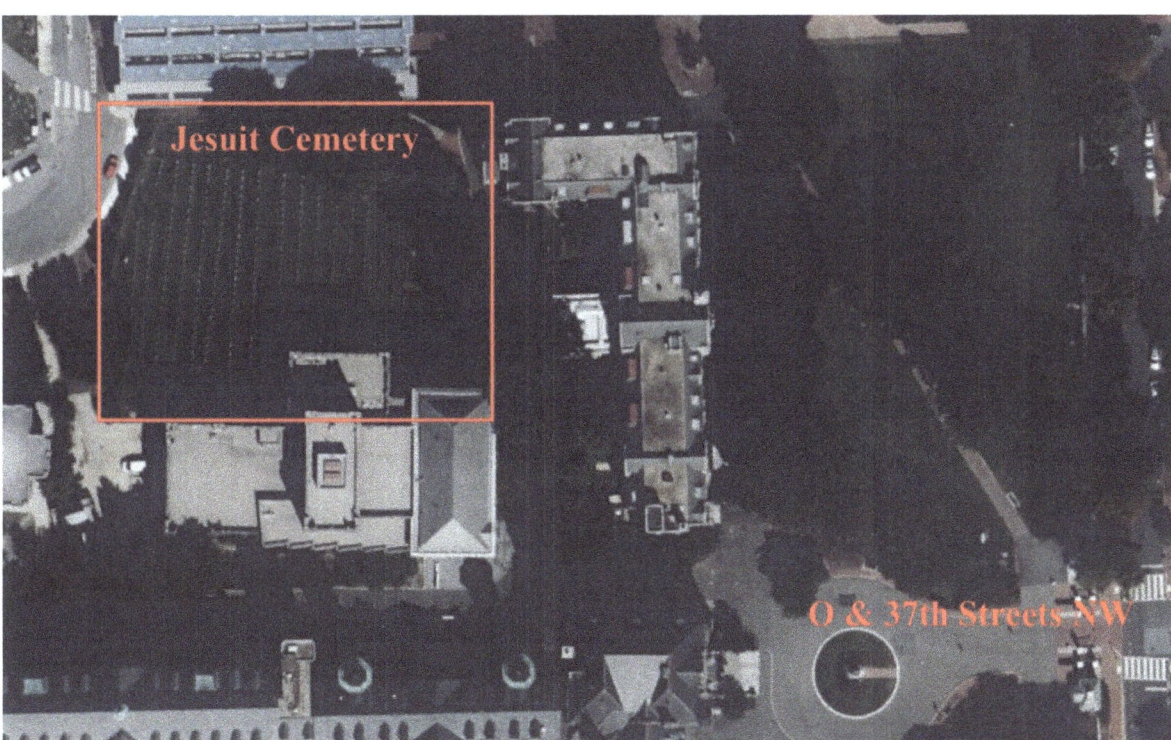

Figure 6 – Signage on West Side of the Jesuit Cemetery

Holy Trinity Parish Cemeteries

There have been a series of parish cemeteries associated with the Holy Trinity Parish, which was established in 1792 by the Jesuits who established Georgetown College.

1. Burials in the Graveyard around the original church building
2. Burials in the Old College Burial Ground also known as Holy Trinity Cemetery #2

3. Burials in Holy Rood Cemetery

Holy Trinity Graveyard

Like many church cemeteries in 18th Century – the burials were initially on the grounds of the church. The church was opened in 1794 on N Street NW and by the 1850s the community had outgrown it. When planning started in 1849 for a new church building, the remains in the Graveyard were moved to land purchased for that purpose. The original graveyard was where the 1851 church and the 1917 school buildings currently stand on 36th Street.

The 1990s pamphlet associated with the 200th anniversary of the Parish tells the story of the move of the remains.

> *In 1849 it was decided that a new church was needed. As was the custom at the time, the old church had been surrounded by its own burial yard as well as neighboring farm dwellings. To the dismay of many parishioners, the burial yard had to be destroyed for the new building. Another plot of land for a cemetery had previously been acquired in conjunction with the College, but the destruction of the old graves caused great consternation among the people. The corner stone of the "New Church" was laid with great ceremony in 1849 and dedicated on June 13, 1851, Trinity Sunday. … Two stones remain from the old burial yard and can be seen in the convent garden and along the back wall of the convent itself.*

Sluby reports that many remains were moved as early as 1817 to the second Holy Trinity Cemetery:

> *Churchyard burials dating from 1789 were made at Holy Trinity Church, located at 3513 N St., NW. In 1817, these burials were removed to College cemetery, which remained the congregations' preferred cemetery until 1834 when the Jesuits, who presided over Georgetown College and the church, established Holy Rood on Wisconsin Avenue, NW.*[ix]

Fletcher (see Researchers of Note – Page 71) reported in 2002 an interesting story about both a possible earlier graveyard and remains uncovered in 1998

Peter T. Higgins

during a small construction project at the current church / school campus. The following is from a 14-page history Fletcher published in *Newsletter of the Catholic Historical Society of Washington*, Volume X, Number 3, July-September, 2002.[x] The paper is well footnoted and very well done.

> *According to tradition, when the site of Holy Trinity Church was purchased in 1787, it was next to a "small but neat graveyard, the resting place of the first Catholic settlers". How many graves had accumulated in the thirty-six years since Georgetown's founding is not known, but it seems clear that the demand for burial in consecrated ground anticipated organization of the parish. That this graveyard was west of the original church--under what is now the Elementary School and the present church--may be judged by subsequent land purchases, the immediate purpose of which appears to have been to consolidate the church and the neighboring graves.*
>
> *The churchyard that was thus created served Holy Trinity Parish as its only burial ground for thirty years. As no death records have come down to us from those years the total of burials in the churchyard can at best be estimated, but if the number of deaths in the first three decades of the parish were thirty a year--just half the rate recorded in the fourth decade, to err on the safe side--the number, not including those buried before 1787, would be nine hundred. By 1945 there was only evidence for two of these graves.*
>
> *Two of the tombstones at the church can be seen near the sacristy wall, though they are not in their original location. The one next to the North wall is that of Mary, wife of Notley Young, Esq., a sister of Archbishop Carroll, who died January 10, 1815, aged 72; the other, next to the east wall, is that of Mary, wife of Augustus Taney, brother of Chief Justice Taney, who died August 16, 1817, and with her was buried her infant son, Roger Brooke Taney. It is said that these tombstones once were set in the wall of the church. These stones, together with two other fragments that recently turned up, are now at the front of the new St. Ignatius Chapel.*

Anyone who inquires at Holy Trinity about the remainder of the graves in the churchyard is likely to be told that they were removed at some time in the past. No doubt some were; it is not unusual for people to move the remains of their more prestigious ancestors to a better address, if they have the means to do so. But as there are so many people in the ground without descendants that could afford the expense of moving graves, common sense suggests that most people's remains have stayed where they always were. The historian of Holy Trinity does relate that many graves were moved in 1817, but he also reminds us that bodies were still to be found in the churchyard a century later.

Holy Trinity undertook construction of new parish facilities in its churchyard in 1998. Although the press was informed that the cemetery had been moved long ago, contractors were advised to watch for bones as they dug. It was not long before evidence of the churchyard's prior use came to light. The only account given to the press characterized the find as a skull and some small bone fragments, but in the end the remains of forty-four men, women and children were turned over to the DeVol Funeral home.

As required by law, forensic anthropologists surveyed the site, and examined each set of remains. Analysis of buttons suggested that two individuals had been buried between 1837 and 1865. At least one man was of African descent. Some remains showed signs that they had been disturbed once before, during an earlier extension of the church. As each day of interrupted work cost ten thousand dollars, there was understandable pressure to conclude the investigation, so graves that were discovered to be lower than the basement of the new building--not to mention graves beyond the perimeter of the excavation--were left where they were.

The Old College Burial Ground (also Known as Holy Trinity Cemetery #2)

In 1817 the remains in the Church Graveyard were moved to a new parish cemetery on the Georgetown University campus across from today's Reiss Science Building. Figure 7, a clipping from Apple maps, is annotated with the location of the cemetery as Holy Trinity Cemetery #2. This image also shows the nearby New Cemetery associated with the Visitation Monastery.

Figure 7 – Map of Holy Trinity Cemetery #2 & Visitation New Cemetery

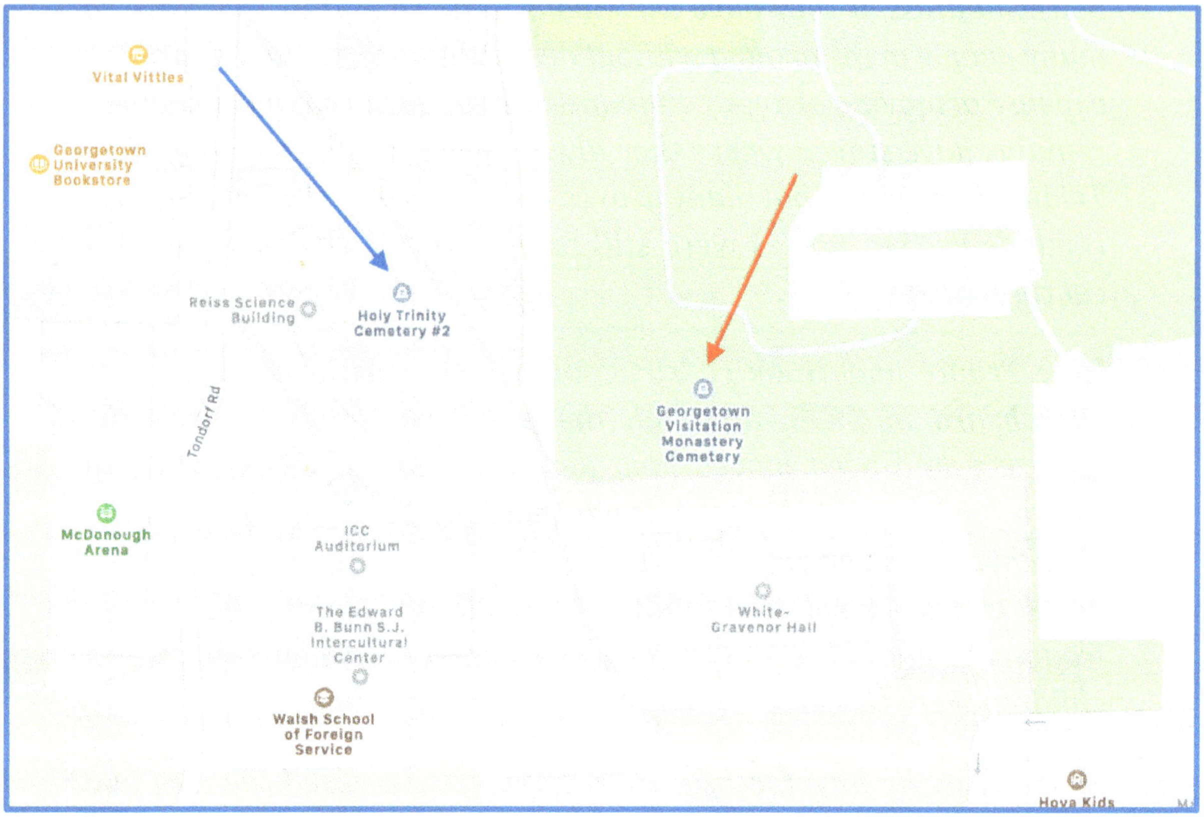

The Holy Trinity Cemetery #2 was closed in 1952 and all of those interred were moved to Mt. Olivet Cemetery in NE Washington. Starting in 1834 burials associated with the Holy Trinity parish were at the Holy Rood Cemetery.

There are several variations of the history of Holy Trinity Cemetery #2 as the web site www.findagrave.com states:

> *Note: one source says this graveyard was also known as 'the College Graveyard'. Others say it was once part of the nearby Holy Trinity Catholic church and this cemetery was said to be the 2nd one used before they bought the larger Holy Rood cemetery on Wisconsin Ave. Several websites and blogs detail the many stories concerning this and the others; used for this description, notes were gleaned from The Georgetown Voice blog and the Glover Park History website.*

Buried in Georgetown

When construction began in 1931 for a new dormitory (Copley Hall), workers found the remnants of it about 100 ft north of the new building. To say that it was overgrown with weeds, broken markers, and other assorted debris is a mild description. Today, the Reiss Science Center sits atop this area. This means it is not to be confused with several other known and well-kept burial sites on the campus grounds today. According to the sources noted above, those once buried here are said to have later been removed to the Mt. Olivet cemetery in the N.E. section of Washington, D.C. Other stories say most were removed to Holy Rood cemetery not too far away. Still, there remain some reports that say few were ever removed and were just bulldozed over and forgotten.[xi]

This second burial ground of Holy Trinity Church was located a few blocks north and west of the church, at the western terminus of Third Street (now P Street), near the southwestern corner of the grounds of Visitation Monastery. Although sometimes this second burial ground was known as the Trinity Burial Ground, or the Old Burying Ground, it was best known as the College Ground.

The most revered grave in the College Ground was that of Susan Decatur, the widow of naval hero Stephen Decatur. A few years after her husband's death she converted to Catholicism, and, at a moment when Georgetown College was in great need, advanced the equivalent of three million dollars [in today's money]. Her house stood about where White-Gravenor Hall is now located on the college campus, and when she died in 1860, she was laid to rest in the Fenwick family lot, just steps from where she had lived.

Decatur is not the only famous name associated with the College Ground, the Death Register of Holy Trinity (the first entry is from December 8, 1818) does contain other items of interest to include the burial of Captain Henry Carbery and his spouse, Sybilla Carbery:

Captain Carbery served in the Revolutionary War, at the end of which he led his men in a march on the capital––Philadelphia, at the time––to demand their back pay. Congress felt threatened, and Carbery was accused of treason. The incident is said to have influenced the determination that the permanent national capital be governed by

> *Congress. Exonerated, Carbery married Sybilla Schneitzel of Frederick, and lived out his days at* Cincinnati, *his farm on Foxhall Road.*
>
> *Carbery, Henry, who died on the 25th inst. (May 27, 1822).*
>
> *Mrs. Sybilla Carbery, who died on the 3d instant suddenly, was buried in the college ground near her husband. (April 6, 1840)*[xii]

Holy Rood Cemetery

In 1832 the Holy Trinity Church purchased land for a new cemetery on the west side of Wisconsin Avenue and of 35th Street. That area was part of Beatty [sometimes spelled Beattie] & Hawkins Addition to Georgetown. The Cemetery called Holy Rood was initially known as the Trinity Church Upper Grave Yard, the location is marked in Figure 8.

Interestingly, all of the street names shown on this 1974 map have changed and the area is no longer in Georgetown, as this part of *Beatty & Hawkins Addition to Georgetown* is now called Glover Park, which starts at what was called Madison Street.

Madison Street is now Whitehaven Parkway and Back Street is Tunlaw Road, which dead ends before Whitehaven. Looking back in time, via Carlton Fletcher's research, we see that the entrance to Holy Rood was originally from Back Street.

> *Behind the* Beatty and Hawkins *lots on the west side of Wisconsin Avenue was* **Back Street**. *The name is self-explanatory, and not unique; it is also the earliest name for Q Street in Georgetown.*
>
> *The northern end of Back Street was at the bend in Tunlaw Road above Davis Place. At its southern end Back Street intersected with what is now Whitehaven Parkway. To the north and east of the latter intersection was* Trinity Church Upper Grave Yard, *which, during the first two decades of its existence--before it was enlarged, and renamed Holy Rood--fronted on Back Street, and had its entrance there.* [xiii]

Figure 8 – Location of Holy Rood Cemetery on an 1874 Map

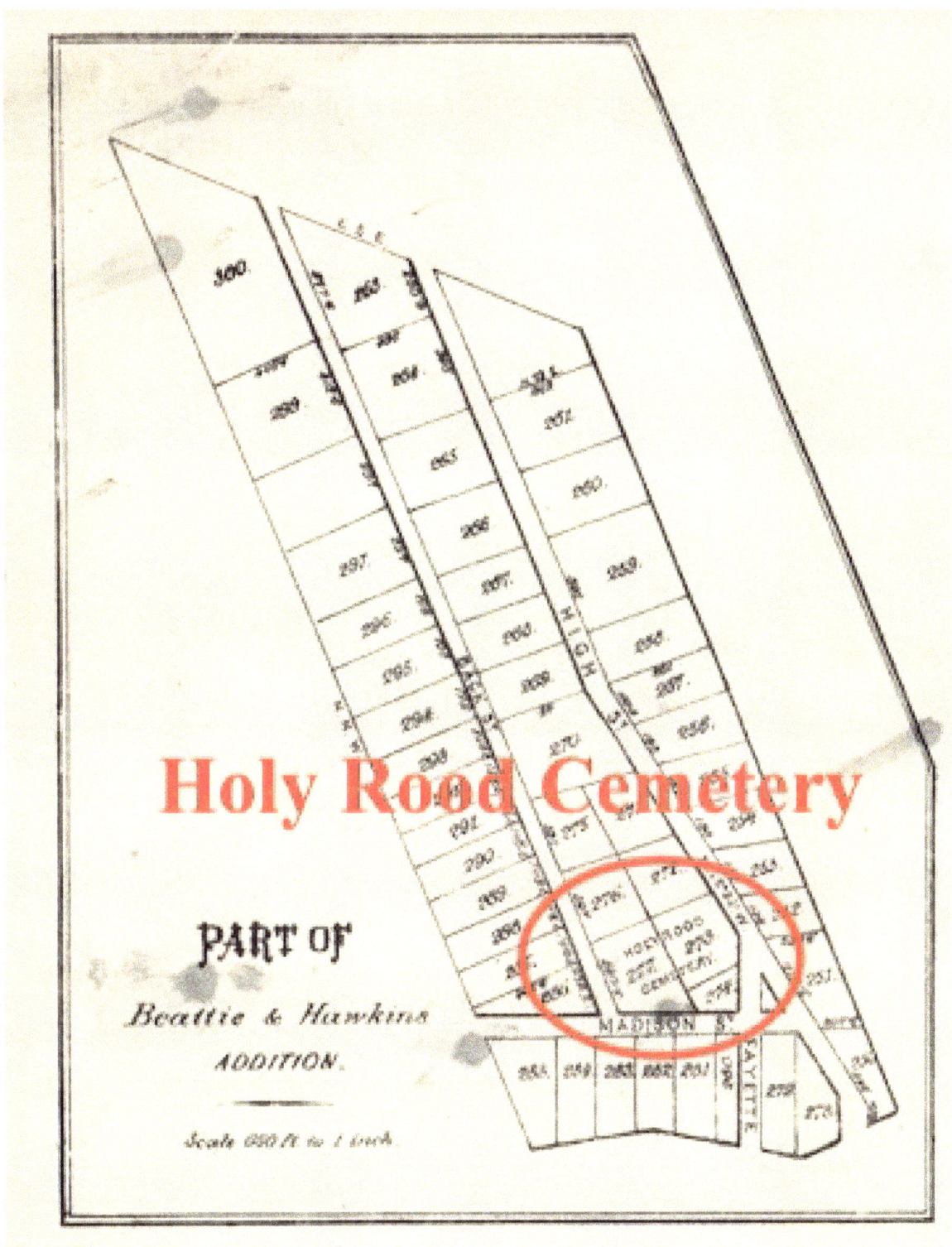

When the first part was purchased in 1832 it was originally referred to as the new or "upper" graveyard, distinguishing it from the older cemeteries on the church proper and the parish's burial grounds on the Georgetown University campus. Additional parcels of land were added to the cemetery in 1853.

In 1925 the Black members of the Holy Trinity decided to create a Catholic Church Parish in Georgetown without the segregation in seating and with full participation in response to what they were experiencing at Holy Trinity. These were the same reasons that had previously driven several Black congregants to spin off from Protestant churches in Georgetown. They formed the Epiphany Catholic Church at 2712 Dumbarton Street. However, they continued to use Holy Rood Cemetery.

Holy Rood Cemetery and the combined Mt. Zion Cemetery have the largest number of free and enslaved Africans buried in Washington, DC. The history is nicely summed up on this sign, Figure 9, that was installed in late 2014 or early 2015.

Figure 9 – Holy Rood Cemetery Sign

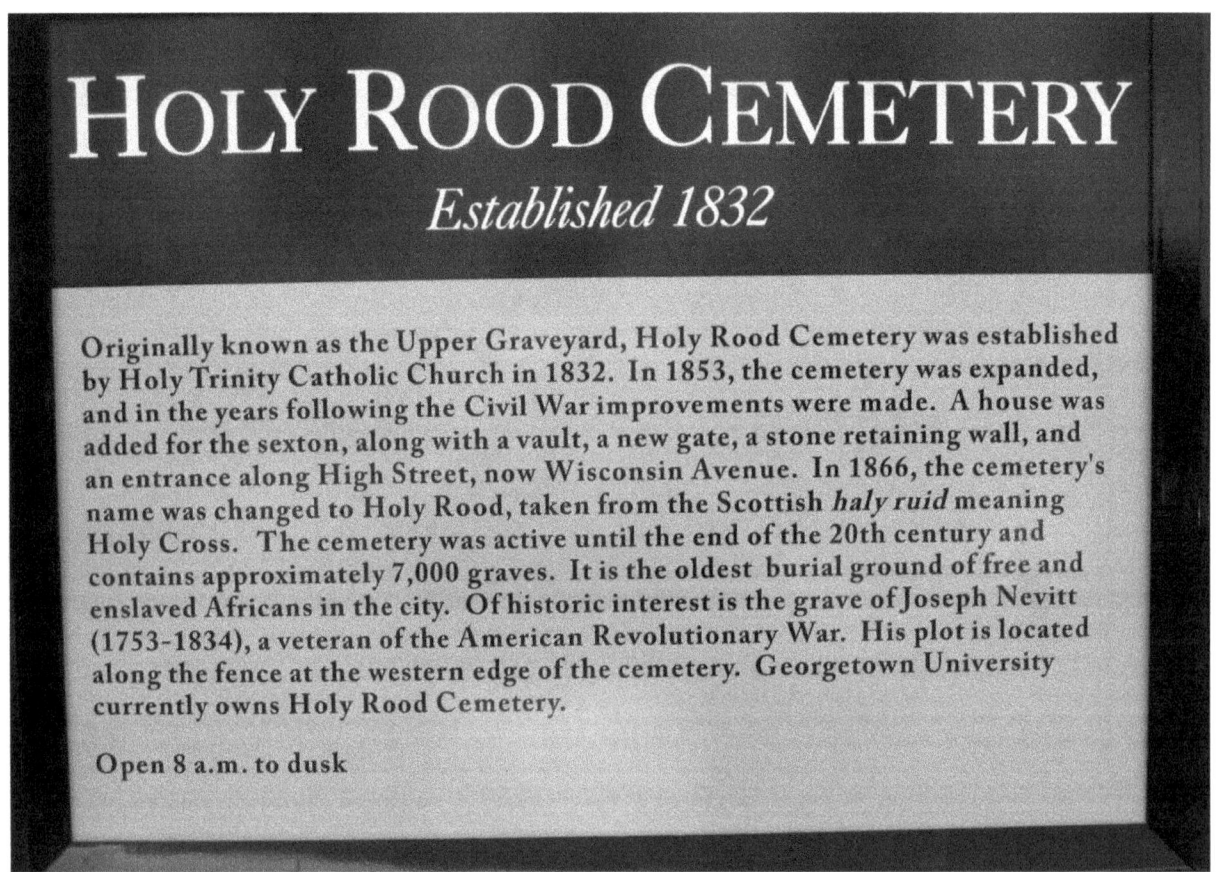

Carlton Fletcher in The Glover Park History web site adds some history to substantiate the information on the sign above.

> *The northwest corner of Holy Rood Cemetery, where there are no grave markers, is, in all likelihood, where the graves are most numerous. This was the "Free Burial Ground" of what was originally called Trinity Church Upper Grave Yard, set aside for burial of the poor; and here lie hundreds of parishioners of Holy Trinity Church in Georgetown who could not afford the price of burial, muchless [sic] stone memorials.*
>
> *This field was also, almost certainly, where those parishioners of Holy Trinity were buried who were enslaved. And, because some of the entries in the Death Registers of Holy Trinity include the surnames of some of the deceased slaves--which is precious information--Holy Rood Cemetery is the best documented slave burial ground in the District of Columbia.*
>
> *As the practice of noting whether the deceased parishioner had been a slave was discontinued in 1841, the total number of slaves buried can only be estimated. Based on the number of slaves-- approximately 36--buried in seven years, the number of slaves buried in Holy Rood Cemetery while slavery existed is sure to exceed one hundred.* [xiv]

In the 1930s, the Jesuits relinquished jurisdiction of the cemetery to the archdiocese, which subsequently turned it over to Georgetown University. By 1984, the University decided to close the cemetery and thereafter restricted interments to current site owners. Georgetown University Library and Archives sources report that over seven thousand have been buried there.

In the latter half of the 2010-2019 decade the Archdiocese, The University, and Holy Trinity Parish agreed on a master plan for maintenance and refurbishment of the Holy Rood Cemetery as well as a plan for adding a columbarium. In late 2019 Holy Trinity dedicated a new columbarium that consists of some 99 niches in the old vault and 546 in a purpose-built, curved wall. The dedication included a history card, a portion of it is shown in Figure 10. The granite wall is shown in Figure 11.

Figure 10 – The Columbarium Construction Report from the Dedication

Construction to Date

Significant progress has been made in 2019 on this ambitious undertaking to reconnect the Holy Trinity congregation to Holy Rood, and offer a final resting place for parishioners and others. Visible today is the Holy Trinity Columbarium, consisting of two components. First the historic brownstone crypt has been restored and 99 columbarium niches have been installed in the interior. Next, seven external panels have been constructed, on a new curved granite wall, containing 546 columbarium niches. Each of the niches in the crypt and in the wall can hold up to two urns. By October 2019, 180 niches have been sold.

Figure 11 – Picture of Holy Rood Columbarium Granite Wall

The Methodist Cemetery

This cemetery was typically referred to as the Old Methodist Episcopal Burying Ground and alternatively as The Old Methodist Cemetery. The three acres comprising this site, Squares 1288 and 1289, began as a graveyard about 1772 and originally served the Methodist Missionary Chapel in Georgetown. The burial area is now informally referred to as Mount Zion Cemetery.

We see in HALS No. DC-15 the origins of this cemetery:

> *On October 13, 1808, Ebenezer and Ann Elliason sold three-quarters of an acre of land in eastern Georgetown to the trustees of the Montgomery Street Methodist Church for $500. The deed stated "the land be used as a burying ground and subdivided into 'lots, lanes or alleys of such dimension as they (the trustees) or the majority of them, in their judgment and discretion, shall think best and most convenient for the aforesaid purpose." The graveyard, later known as the Old Methodist Burying Ground, was surveyed in October, 1808, and divided into plots, with the first $500 collected from the sale of these plots used to recoup the purchase price of the cemetery. The only known record of the initial survey indicates that three-quarters of the cemetery was reserved for white burials and the remainder for African Americans, predominately slaves.*[xv]

Mount Zion Cemetery

In 1808 the membership of the Dumbarton Street M.E. Church was fifty percent black, consisting of both free blacks and slaves, while Georgetown itself was about thirty percent Black. In 1813 many of the Black members split off from the Dumbarton Street M.E. Church to form the Mt. Zion Methodist Church.[xvi]

Figure 12 – Mt. Zion Cemetery / FUB Cemetery History Plaque

As the sign in Figure 12 states, two cemeteries were associated with the Mt. Zion Church land:

1. The Methodist Georgetown Cemetery which was generally called Old Methodist Burying Ground - to the east. Originally owned by the Dumbarton Street Methodist Church.
2. The Female Union Band (now often referred to as FUB) Cemetery - to the west.

The Old Methodist Episcopal Burying Ground

On October 13, 1808, the trustees of the Montgomery Street Church (successor to the Methodist Missionary Chapel), known as Dumbarton Methodist Church after 1850, purchased this property on Mill Road near 25th and Q Streets, NW, to serve as a church burial ground. For the next forty years, this cemetery served the biracial congregation. However, neighboring Oak Hill was chartered in 1849 and became the favored local interment area. This resulted with only infrequent use of the Old Methodist grounds. Dumbarton Church sold the western section to the Female Union Band Society in 1842 and, in 1874, leased the remaining portion to Mt. Zion Methodist Church for 99 years. Currently the site is managed by the Mt. Zion/Female Union Band Historic Memorial Park, Inc., a Foundation. White burials continued in the property until after the Civil War, although they decreased in numbers after Oak Hill Cemetery opened in 1849. Between 1849 and 1892, several White graves were disinterred and moved; most of those were re-buried at Oak Hill.

The Old Methodist Episcopal Burying Ground is now part of the Mount Zion Cemetery complex. African-American members of Mount Zion were buried in the remaining available sections and in the plots left open by the White disinterments. The last burial was in 1950.

The Female Union Band Society Graveyard

The Mount Zion United Methodist Church also took over the Female Union Band Society Graveyard (or Cemetery). Over time, these two contiguous cemeteries have become known simply as the Mount Zion Cemetery. The combined cemetery fell into neglect and disrepair, leading to a 1953 DC government prohibition against additional burials in the FUB. There was a legal battle on and off until the 1970s between factions that wanted to sell and the historically minded families.[xvii]

As a single unit, the cemetery was added to the National Register of Historic Places in 1975. At that time Paul Sluby researched the Old Methodist Burying Ground, his report is available through the Genealogical Department of the Church of Jesus Christ of Latter-Day Saints.[xviii] This ended the legal battle.

The lack of maintenance continued until 1976 when volunteer workers under the direction of the Afro-American Bicentennial Corporation[xix] cleared away underbrush, trash, and ground cover. The tombstones have mostly been knocked about and the cleanup led to them being placed in clusters but most were not reassembled. Figure 13 is from a DC Preservation League advertisement for an October 2021 tour of these cemeteries – led by the Mt. Zion/Female Union Band Historic Memorial Park, Inc.

The two original, adjacent cemeteries are located on the north side of (dead end) Mill Street, off 27th Street just north of Q Street. Mill Street fed into Lyons Mill Road that went down the embankment to Lyons Mill across Rock Creek. Figure 14 shows the location of the joint cemeteries just to the east of Lyons Mill Road (now a foot path) and Oak Hill Cemetery on the west side of Lyons Mill Road – shown as 27th street in the Figure.

Figure 13 – Mt Zion & FUB Cemetery Picture

Buried in Georgetown

Figure 14 – Plat of Mt. Zion Cemetery

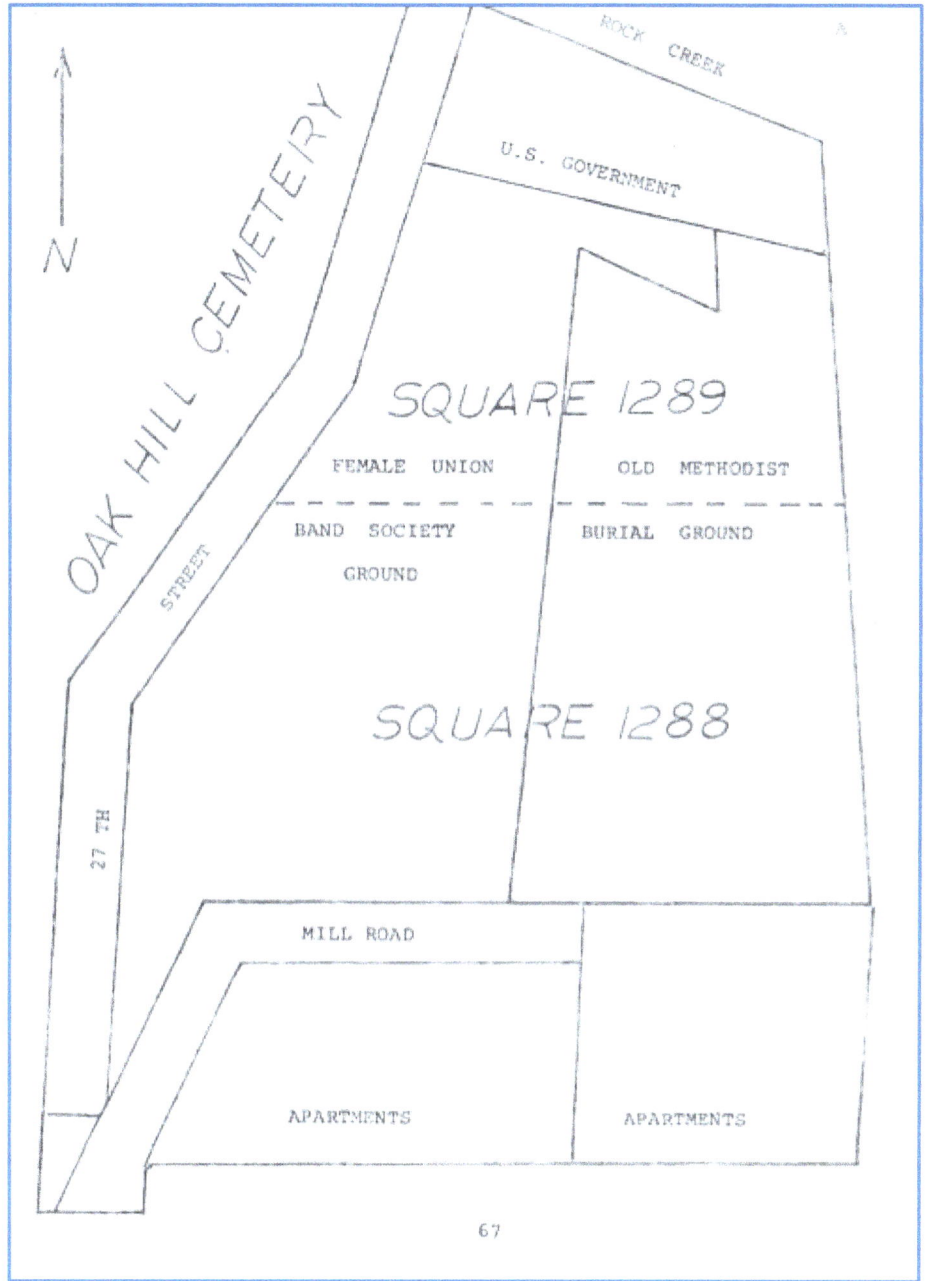

These two adjacent cemeteries (FUB & Old Methodist) were recognized by the UNESCO Slave Route Project. The story was reported by The Washington Informer on December 19, 2018. The story is quoted here as it is very relevant to the racial history currently being updated and shared relative to Georgetown's enslaved and freed Blacks' relations with churches & cemeteries in the 19th and 20th Centuries.

Peter T. Higgins

More than 75 people recently gathered in Georgetown to remember and honor the ancestors buried in two historic African-American cemeteries — Mount Zion Church cemetery and the adjacent Female Union Band Society (FUBS) cemetery.

The combined three-acre, grassy and tree-lined properties, tucked away at 27th Street and Mill Road NW bordering Rock Creek Park, were recognized as an associated Site of Memory of the United Nations Educational, Scientific and Cultural Organization (UNESCO) Slave Route Project. The decree is the first such designation in D.C. and first such U.N. recognition of cemeteries.

The Mount Zion and Female Union Band Society Cemeteries are two of the oldest remaining Black cemeteries in Georgetown and greater D.C., dating from 1809 to the 1950s. The properties are also a National Underground Railroad Network to Freedom site and listed on the National Register of Historic Places.

In honor of the acknowledgement, the Mt. Zion Church – FUBS Cemetery Memorial Park Foundation hosted a free public lecture series, "Black Georgetown Remembered," at the Dumbarton House with historian, lecturer and author C.R. Gibbs, who also has a book by the same name.

"We are honored that the cemeteries and those interred are receiving international recognition of their historical importance as a site of memory of the UNESCO Slave Route Project," said Neville Waters III, president of the foundation's board. "We hope this encourages more people to visit the cemetery and support our efforts to preserve this important history by designing a memorial park and educational programs."

The two neighboring cemeteries recall African Americans that helped build the prosperous Georgetown neighborhood and later the city of Washington. Slave ships embarked from West Africa brought Africans to the Port of Georgetown in the 1700s. Georgetown's residents included both enslaved and free Blacks, many whom attended Montgomery Street Church (now Dumbarton United

Methodist), Georgetown's first Methodist Church. Deceased parishioners, White and Black, were buried in the Old Methodist Burying Ground.

In 1816, 100 Black members, tired of the church's segregation practices, withdrew to form a separate congregation, Mt. Zion United Methodist Church (now located at 1334 29th Street NW), the city's oldest Black congregation. The new church flourished despite the loss of some congregants noted in the registry as "sold to Georgia trader" or "escaped."

In 1842, a group of free Black women calling themselves the Female Union Band Society bought the property adjacent to the Old Methodist Burying Ground for the burial of freed African Americans. The Female Union Band Society was a benevolent association and offered both pension and burial benefits to its members. The creation of the all-White Oak Hill Cemetery in 1849 immediately west of the Female Union Band Cemetery led to numerous disinterments of White burials in the Old Methodist Burying Ground.

After 30 years of increasingly infrequent use, Montgomery Street Methodist Church (known as the Dumbarton Street Methodist Church after 1850) granted a 99-year lease of the Methodist grounds to Mount Zion Church.

Mt. Zion Church and other Black churches in D.C. were keenly aware of the 1848 Pearl Affair, the largest attempted escape of enslaved persons by water on the Underground Railroad. Over 70 enslaved persons sought freedom on the schooner the Pearl that embarked from D.C.'s Southwest waterfront and sailed down the Potomac River. But slaveowners overtook the ship, caught the freedom seekers and sold them back into slavery, sparking riots in D.C.

Elizabeth Edmonson Brent, the eldest sister of Mary and Emily Edmonson, two of the Pearl Affair's freedom-seekers and inspiration for the book "Uncle Tom's Cabin," was also the wife of John Brent, a prayer leader at Mt. Zion Church. After the Pearl Affair, there were calls for Georgetown to retrocede to Maryland to protect slaveholding interests. The Pearl Affair also contributed to the Compromise of 1850, which abolished slave trading in D.C. and defused a four-year political confrontation between slaveholding and free states.

President Abraham Lincoln signed the District of Columbia Emancipation Act into law on April 16, 1862, which ended slavery in the nation's capital.

The UNESCO Slave Route Project encourages new research in neglected regions and defines new approaches in teaching, preserving and promoting history and historical sites related to the slave trade. It also aims to promote the contributions of people of African descent to the establishments of contemporary societies and preserve written archives and intangible heritage related to history.

Plans for a spring 2019 formal dedication is underway.[xx]

Oak Hill Cemetery

William Wilson Corcoran established the Oak Hill Cemetery in memory of his wife, Louise, who died at the age of twenty-one. Oak Hill is now at 3001 R Street east of Wisconsin Ave, which was known as Road Street in 1849. Congress approved the charter for the 15-acre Cemetery on March 3, 1849, with dedication of the cemetery that July 4th.[xxi]

There are a number of pre-1849 graves in the cemetery, mostly those who were originally buried in either the Methodist or Presbyterian cemeteries in Georgetown and disinterred and reburied at Oak Hill after 1849.[xxii]

The cemetery's web site provides a nice historical perspective:

In the center of Georgetown, lying along Rock Creek, a neighbor of Dumbarton Oaks (where John C. Calhoun lived while in the Senate) and of Evermay, is a 19th Century garden park cemetery rivaled only by Boston's Mount Auburn Cemetery in graciousness and a sense of community.

The Oak Hill Cemetery was founded by Mr. W.W. Corcoran. Mr. Corcoran was a banker and co-founder of what was The Riggs National Bank. He may have kept the Union Treasury solvent in the Mexican War by persuading the British to buy U.S. bonds. He was a man of many tastes and philanthropies (e.g. the Corcoran Gallery; the Louise Home). In 1848, Mr. Corcoran purchased 15 acres along Rock Creek from George Corbin Washington (a distinguished lawyer and a great nephew of the First President) and his son Lewis W. Washington. When the Cemetery Company was incorporated by Act of Congress on March 3, 1849, Mr. Corcoran contributed the land to the Company. Captain George F. de la Roche, a master engineer, supervised the grading, including the creation of a grand bank along Rock Creek, and the plotting. James Renwick, Jr., architect of the Smithsonian Building and of the original Corcoran Gallery which is now the Renwick Gallery, designed the iron enclosure and the Chapel (built in 1849) which is a representation of the finest English specimens of old Gothic chapels. The cemetery itself is a major example of the 19th Century Romantic movement, the natural and not formal English garden, an acceptance and blending of nature rather than a geometrical imposition.

Because of Oak Hill's age, its history is largely 19th Century, with emphasis on the great Civil War. All lots were sold long ago and, until recently, the only new interments possible were in the few spaces remaining in old family lots. Recently, a new project has been started to renovate the paths and walkways. In this manner, new interment spaces are being made available. Thus, Oak Hill will be a neighborhood garden with a continuing history.[xxiii]

Figure 15 – Willow Columbarium at Oak Hill

In the early 22nd Century Oak Hill added several additional columbarium sites in various locations in the cemetery to include footpaths. The largest of these is the Willow Columbarium, pictured in Figure 15.

Figure 16 – Renwick Chapel at Oak Hill

This cemetery is the only Georgetown cemetery discussed in the Society of Architectural Historians' Buildings of the District of Columbia (Pages 414 & 415). The Cemetery Gatehouse and the Cemetery Chapel are both included in the 1993 volume, the Renwick designed chapel can be seen in Figure 16.

With so many new burial sites for cremains, particularity along the walkways, there is a real chance for families to inject their feelings, to include humor. The cleverest memorial message experienced in researching this book was at Oak Hill – see Figure 17. The family, Roselee and William "Art" Roberts, clearly had a great sense of humor. Reading her obituary, I see that she was remarkably successful in several fields including chief aide on the House Budget Committee. Their boat was cleverly named *MissAppropriation*. Having lived in Georgetown, their family plaque on a sidewalk stone / columbarium marker makes a point that so many of us can appreciate – *We found a place to park in Georgetown!*

Figure 17 – Humorous Burial Marker

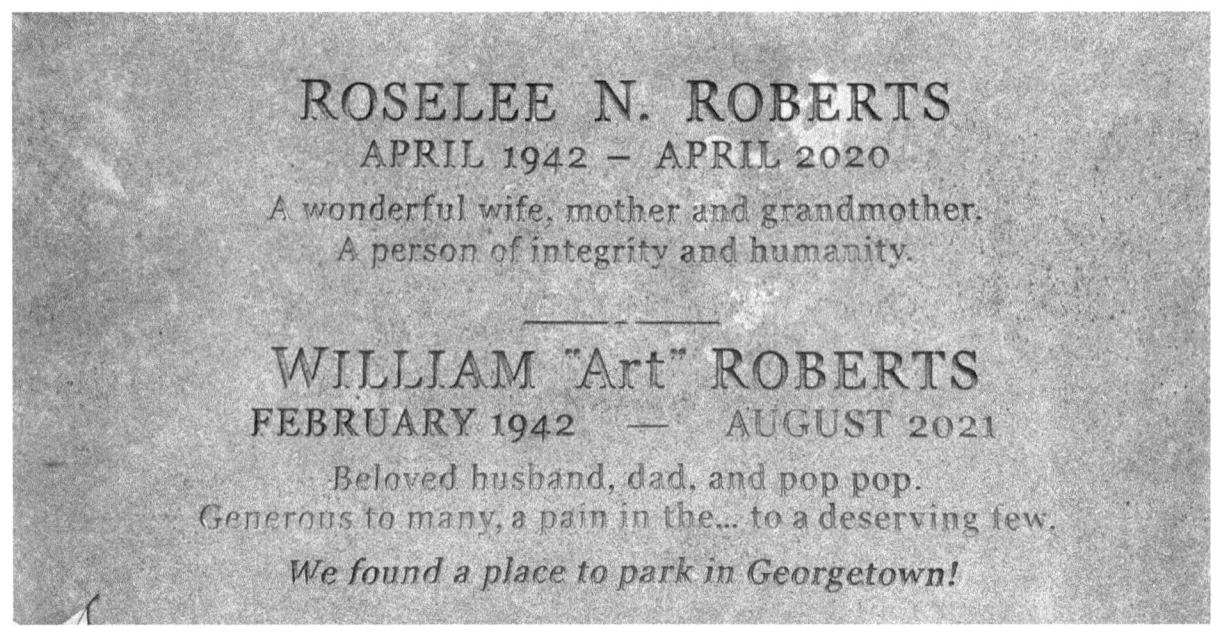

Presbyterian Church Cemeteries

The first church building was on Bridge Street the church was known as the Bridge Street Presbyterian Church. There were two cemeteries associated with this Georgetown Presbyterian congregation as well as a chapel on 33rd Street (formerly Market Street) at the Burial Ground:

1. The Bridge Street Presbyterian Graveyard (On Bridge Street)
2. The Presbyterian Burial Ground (In the block bounded by 4th, 5th, Market, and Fredericks Streets)

The Bridge Street Presbyterian Graveyard

This church was at the southeast corner of what is now 30th and M Streets. A graveyard occupied the lawn to the east of the church building.[xxiv] When the church was razed in the early part of 1873 the bodies were reinterred in the Presbyterian Burial Ground on 33rd Street (at the time - Market Street).[xxv] The location of their first church on Bridge Street is marked on Figure 18 below, the 1851 map shows the church as a black rectangle.

Figure 18 – Location of the Presbyterian Church & Graveyard on Bridge Street

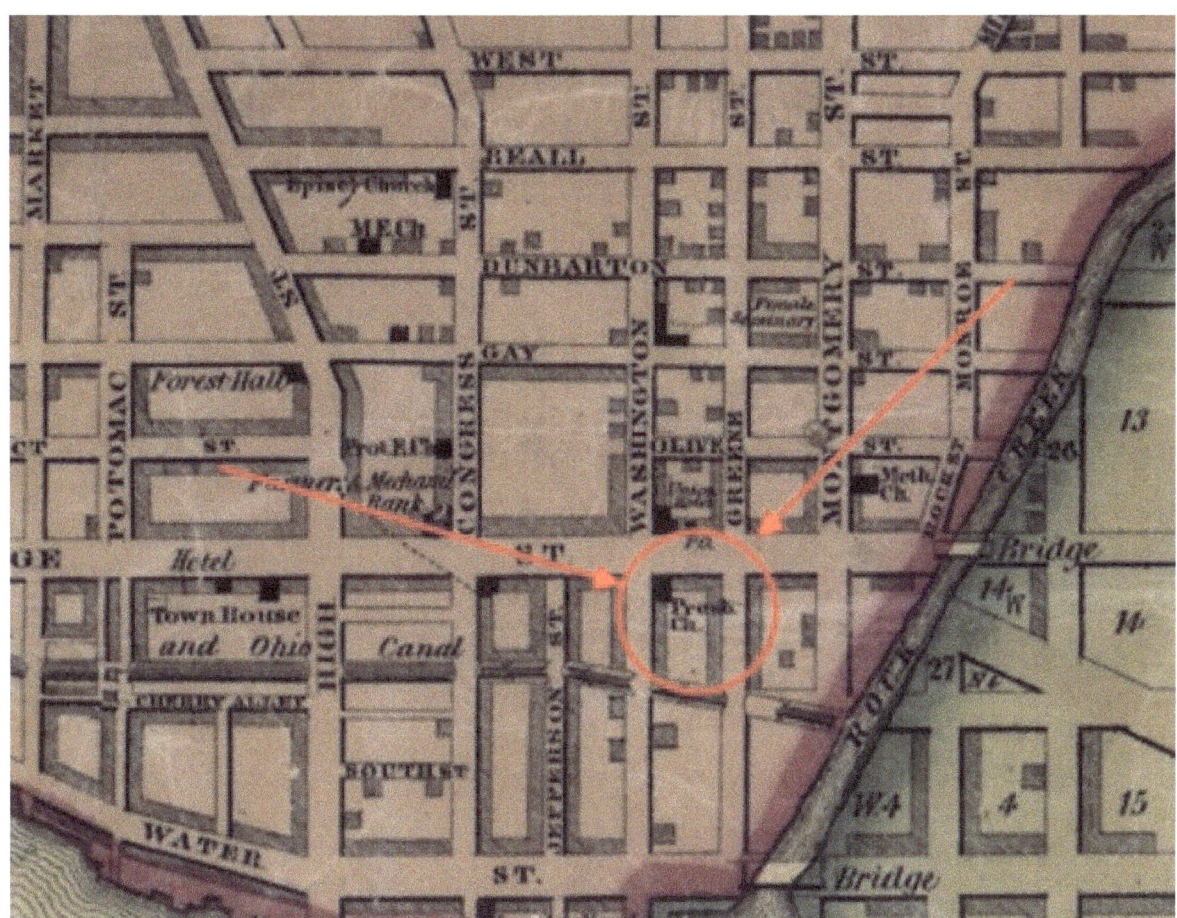

On 22 August 1802 the Georgetown Presbyterian Church on Bridge Street purchased land for a larger Burial Ground in the block bounded by 4th, 5th, Market, and Fredericks Streets. This decision was a result of a need for more space for burials than available in their existing Bridge Street Graveyard. They started internments at the Burial Ground in 1804. The 1802 event has been researched and documented by Carlton Fletcher, quoting from an 1802 newspaper article:

> *The committee of the Presbyterian congregation in George-Town, wishing to discontinue the interment of the dead in the burying ground next to the church, have lately purchased a large plat of land, for the purpose of a grave yard, which is a beautiful eminence, situated between the Columbian Academy and Mr. Threlkeld's Meadow Farm. Part of this purchase has been paid off by Mr. Fenwick, and divided into small lots suitable for the interment of whole families: the committee, therefore, wish immediately to sell as*

> *many of these lots, as will raise a fund sufficiently large to enclose the ground with a decent pole and rail fence and liquidate what of the purchase money remains as yet unpaid. Let all who wish to see the plat of the graveyard and to become purchasers, make application to Thomas Corcoran, or to Mr. James Melvin, Bridge Street, George-Town. N.B. Lots at present will be sold low for cash, in order to defray present expenses, but when these are discharged, they will rise much higher in price. (Washington Federalist, Georgetown, D.C., September 1, 1802)*[xxvi]

The Find a Grave website provides interesting details of Balch's life including that his remains were reinterred at Oak Hill Cemetery (Chapel Hill, Lot 632 ¼) in 1874.

> *Balch was a Presbyterian Minister, Educator, Revolutionary War Officer. He graduated from the College of New Jersey (now Princeton University) in 1774 and became head of the Lower Marlborough Academy in Calvert County, Maryland. During the Revolution he served as a Captain and led a charge of students on missions that harassed the British along the Chesapeake Bay and Patuxent River, a strategy that the more famous Joshua Barney would copy during the War of 1812. In 1780, Balch established Georgetown Presbyterian Church, which was the second church in Georgetown (now part of Washington, DC). He also served as headmaster of the Columbian Academy in Georgetown. Bio by Fred Sanford.*[xxvii]

The Presbyterian Burial Ground

The Presbyterian Burial Ground, the land having been purchased in 1802, existed until 1906. On October 4, 1942, The Sunday Star, Washington, a DC newspaper, in possibly the longest sentence ever published, reported:

> *"This God's acre was laid out by the congregation of the Bridge Street Presbyterian Church in 1802, of which the Reverend Stephen Bloomer Balch, D. D., was the first pastor, serving from 1780 to the time of his death in 1833, when his remains were placed in the wall of the church, and removed from therein 1873 by Joseph F. Birch, an early Georgetown undertaker, and interred in the church graveyard*

on Q Street, and from there it was removed the following year, through the beneficence of the philanthropist, W. W. Corcoran, to Oak Hill Cemetery, and today the same tablet that was placed by the family in October 1835, in front of the church he founded, now covers his last resting place and reads:

Sacred to the memory of

STEPHEN BALCH, D. D.

Who died September 22, 1833,

in the 87th year of his age.

He was the founder of this church

and for more than half a century

its reverend pastor.

He planted the gospel in this town

and his example was for many

a light to its inhabitants.

He being dead, yet speaketh.

Stephen Bloomer Balch was an American patriot – no clergyman should be less. At the top of his grave is the War Department's stone that tells a story every son of a Revolutionary soldier to read. It simply but eloquently states:

Capt. Steven B. Balch

Calvert Co., MD., Mil. Rev. War.

In 1873, the Bridge Street Church moved and was renamed the West Street Presbyterian Church.

This is further embellished by the well footnoted article in Wikipedia.

... Land for both the cemetery and a new Georgetown Presbyterian Church were donated by Dr. Charles Beatty, who provided a building lot of 1,500 square feet (140 m2) on the block. Beatty required that the property be used for either a church or a cemetery, and that the property should revert to Beatty's heirs if not used for either purpose. (Furthermore, the act of Congress of March 28, 1806, under which Georgetown Presbyterian Church was incorporated stipulated that the graveyard could not be used for any other purpose or disposed of.) Dr. Beatty also donated a building lot on the block to the Methodist Episcopal Church, but this land became an annex of cemetery when the Methodists declined to build there. ... The burying ground (the term "cemetery" did not come into use until mid-century) was located in a middle-class neighborhood. ...

Burials began at the cemetery in 1806. In January 1812, lots in the northwest corner of the cemetery were set aside for the burial of African Americans.

Although Presbyterian Burying Ground was beautiful, it did not retain its popularity for long. In 1807, the 35.75-acre (144,700 m2) Congressional Cemetery was established on the east side of the city on the shores of the Anacostia River. Despite being one of the largest cemeteries in the District of Columbia, Presbyterian Burying Ground quickly came to be seen as too small and crowded to permit the construction of the large funerary monuments favored by Americans in the Victorian era. Large, open Congressional Cemetery, however, provided ample land for memorials. As Congressional Cemetery grew in popularity, the Presbyterian Burying Ground fell into disrepair. By 1847, thickets of weeds and shrubs had taken over the cemetery. The cemetery's large public vault, never adequately sealed, reeked of decay.

A fire at the Balch's home destroyed many of cemetery's burial records in 1831.

Another blow to the Presbyterian Burying Ground occurred in 1848, when 12.5 acres (51,000 m2) Oak Hill Cemetery opened just five blocks to the northwest. [Actually, it was opened to the Northeast] This garden cemetery with beautiful landscaping, terraces, spacious grounds, and magnificent chapel—created and financed by the city's richest businessman, William Wilson Corcoran—deeply appealed to the residents of Georgetown and Washington. Over the next several years, Oak Hill became not only the cemetery of choice for new burials, but many families disinterred their loved ones at the Presbyterian Burying Ground and reburied them at Oak Hill. Oak Hill quickly expanded, and by 1867 had more than 25 acres (100,000 m2) of space for burials. Bounded by city streets and existing homes, Presbyterian Burying Ground was limited in size. A large increase in burials at Presbyterian Burying Ground occurred during a cholera epidemic of 1834. Georgetown resident Charles H. Trunnel, who lived during the period, said that the dead were brought to the cemetery in cartloads. The dead arrived in such numbers so quickly that cemetery officials did not keep accurate records as to where corpses were buried. Many bodies were buried in the middle of the streets surrounding the cemetery, because church officials worried about filling the cemetery with cholera victims. Another upsurge in burials occurred during the American Civil War, as they did at all regional cemeteries, but otherwise the number of burials at the cemetery remained fairly constant and low

The new Presbyterian Church was on the west side of 33rd Street (then known as Market Street) and the cemetery occupied about a third of the block, running west, behind the church. The church is now a private residence.[xxviii]

The references to a *Church* in the last two sentences above are not correct, they should refer to a *Chapel*. The Chapel was built in 1855 and sold in 1901.[xxix] This will be explained in the complimentary book: <u>God Lives in Georgetown, A Brief Look at His Many Houses</u>.

The 1887 Hopkins map (shown below as Figure 19 and Figure 20) shows a Presbyterian Chapel adjacent to the cemetery. Figure 19 also shows other points of interest mentioned in this book – to help orient readers who are not familiar with Georgetown. The map shows where the Presbyterian Burial

Ground was located, the west half of this block is now Volta Park. The park's swimming pool is located roughly where the figure "103" is shown on the map. The arrow points to the *Prest CH* label on the map, in block 103. The houses shown on Block 103 in 1887 other than those on 33rd Street, are all gone, removed before the Volta Park was opened.

In the mid-1800s the Burial Ground became overgrown and started to slide into disrepair, as noted in the Wikipedia article quoted above. This eventually led into its closure and sale to the District Government early in the 20th Century.

> *In February 1896, Georgetown Presbyterian Church established a "committee on church property" to dispose of the cemetery. The church agreed to advertise Presbyterian Burying Ground's closure once more, and to demand that all remains be claimed by September 1, 1896. The church agreed that all bodies which went unclaimed would be reinterred at another cemetery at church expense. The church said the property would be subdivided into housing lots and sold.*
>
> *The deterioration of Presbyterian Burying Ground continued into 1896. Local people began using the cemetery as a garbage dump, throwing old wire, pieces of metal, tin cans, carcasses, and household ashes onto the grounds. There were open graves everywhere, and in some cases coffins protruded from the ground. In May 1896, a strong storm blew the roof off the cemetery chapel. Georgetown Presbyterian Church had appointed Andrew Goldsmith sexton of the cemetery, but he was unable to deal with the cemetery's many problems.*
>
> *On September 5, 1896, the Presbyterian Burying Ground trustees announced that, the removal deadline having passed, all remaining bodies at the cemetery would be disinterred and moved to Beechmont Cemetery in Montgomery County, Maryland. But no disinterments occurred. [Apparently that Maryland cemetery was never built.]*
>
> *By the fall of 1898, conditions at Presbyterian Burying Ground had no improved. Georgetown Presbyterian Church no longer had a*

sexton appointed to oversee the grounds, and a rank odor was coming out of many of the open graves. In September 1898, at the behest of Georgetown residents, the City Commissioners of the District of Columbia introduced legislation to make it a crime to allow property to become a public nuisance. Whether the legislation passed or not is unclear, but little was done to rectify the problems at the cemetery.

On December 9, 1898, a road crew working on a street adjacent to Presbyterian Burying Ground unearthed four skeletons. The Washington Post reported that that these were likely victims of the 1834 cholera epidemic. Since the street had been regraded since the burials almost 78 years earlier, many of these bodies were now very close to the surface.

On May 7, 1899, a GCA subcommittee formed to handle cemetery issues issued a report requesting that Presbyterian Burying Ground be turned into a public playground, and that the City Commissioners be prevailed upon to push this legislation in Congress.

...

But despite the GCA's efforts, no action was taken on this legislative initiative. Georgetown Presbyterian Church sold the chapel to the West Washington Methodist Episcopal Church South (an all-black congregation) in 1901. The cemetery's condition in 1901 was very poor. More than 100 vaults had been broken open, all the mausoleums had been looted of their brick and torn down, and headstones scattered widely. Only about 500 to 700 of the 2,700 people buried there had been removed, and half of all burials could not be located because the markers were gone. Some relatives secured a disinterment permit, only to discover that the grave of their loved ones could not be identified. Those who remained belonged to both wealthy and poor families. A great number of remains had been unearthed, and bone fragments lay on the surface of the cemetery.

...

On September 29, 1908, the City Commissioners recommended the purchase of the Presbyterian Burying Ground for $32,000. Some time in late June or early July 1909, the sale finally was consummated for $30,000. The city paid $20,000, while private donations came up with the remaining $10,000.

During preparation of the area for conversion to a playground, 30 more bodies were uncovered. These were sent to an undertaker for cremation and burial. But more than 2,000 corpses remained buried at the site. Noted D.C. historian John Proctor Clagett claimed in 1942 that most of the bodies near 34th Street NW had probably all been removed, but the central, southern, and southeastern portions remained untouched. The total cost of the Georgetown Municipal Playground (now named Volta Park) was $35,000, of which $30,000 was needed for the land and $5,000 for equipment. The new playground opened on October 30, 1909, and proved immediately popular.

Figure 19 – 1887 Map of Georgetown with Several Sites Marked

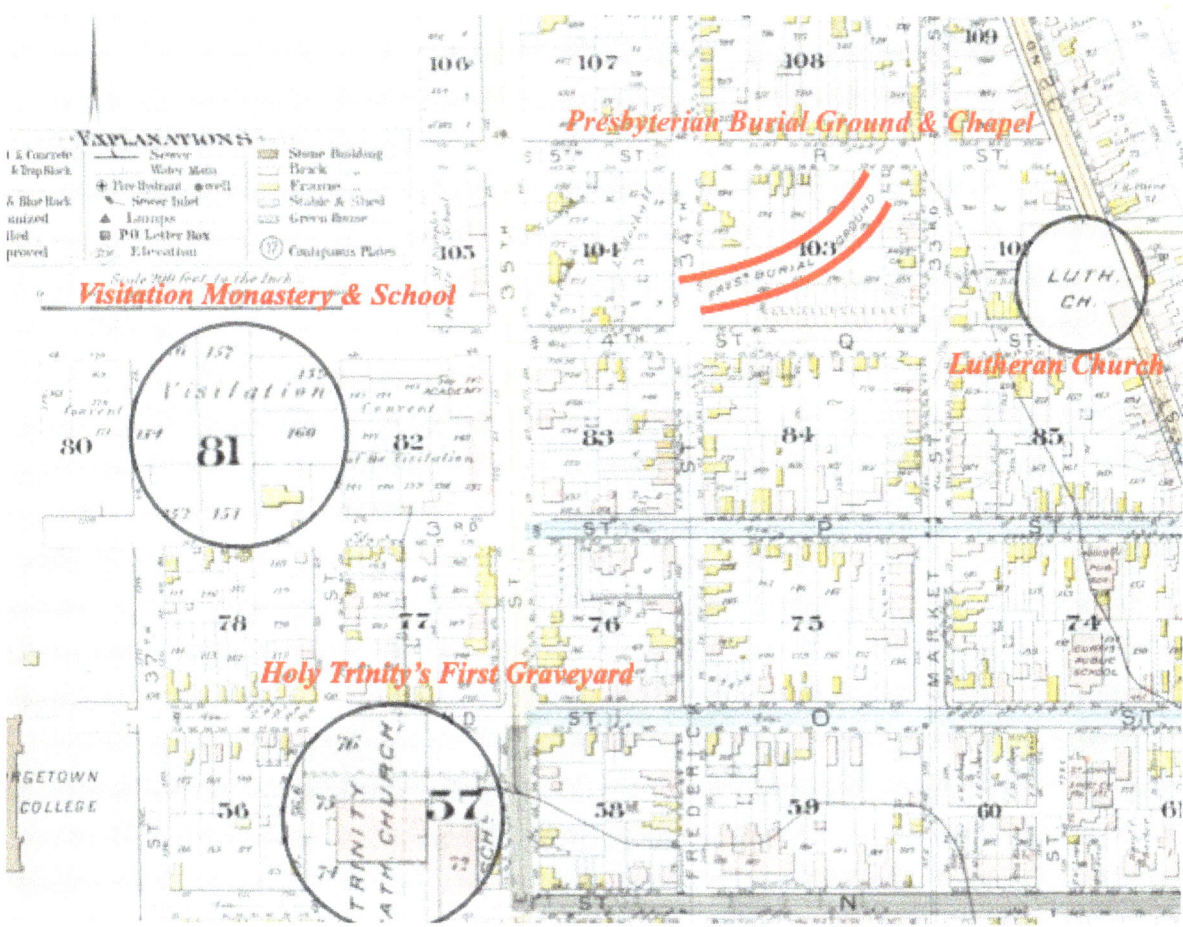

Figure 20 – 1887 Map of Presbyterian Burial Ground and Chapel

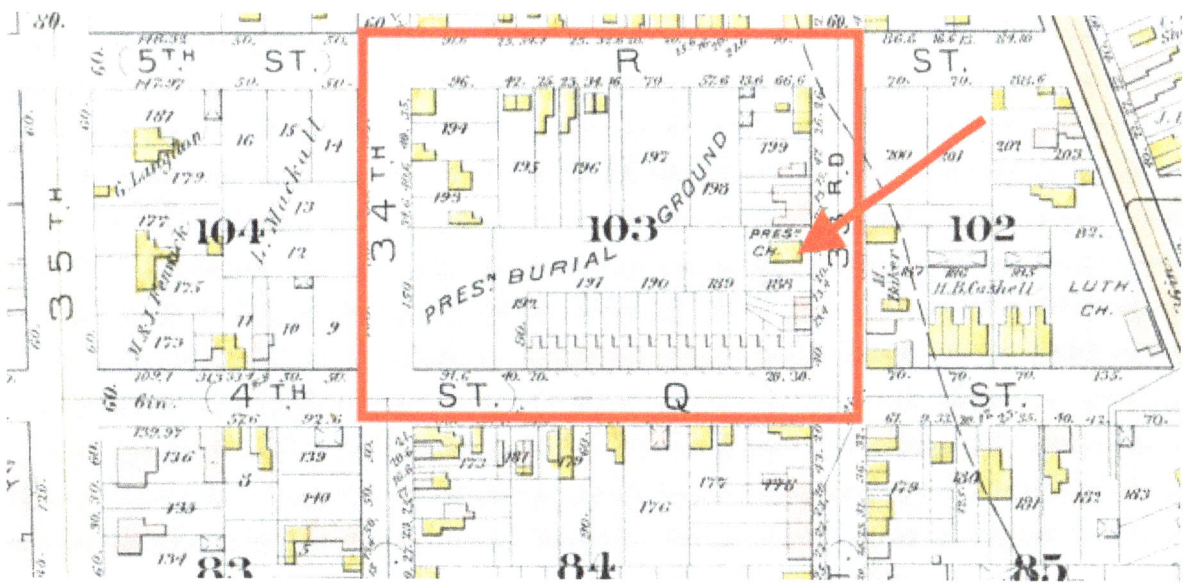

Peter T. Higgins

The Columbian Harmony Society, a mutual aid organization founded in 1825 by a group of free African-Americans, started their own cemetery in Washington in 1929. In 1990 Paul E. Sluby, Sr. and Stanton L. Wormley published a detailed book, under the name of The Columbian Harmony Society, entitled: <u>Presbyterian Cemetery Records (Georgetown) Washington, DC 1856 – 1897</u>. Their book is available at the Georgetown Public Library, Peabody Room

Much of what Messrs. Sluby and Wormley collected and published gives a deep insight into the Presbyterian Burial Ground and the events associated with its successful years. The highlights of their materials are provided here:

- The Presbyterian Cemetery of Georgetown was established in 1802 as a modest churchyard burial area.

- Originally the cemetery was for the exclusive use of the Presbyterian Church of Georgetown. This was relaxed and just 10 years later sixteen lots were reserved for persons of colour (sic) – all in the original 1802 cemetery.

- Early on there was a need to expand and the congregation purchased the land known as the Presbyterian Burial Grounds – see Figure 20, above, from 1887.

- The early records from the cemetery are all lost – the actual detailed recording of burials is available only back to 1856 – about 30 years after the property was acquired. Estimates range between 700 to 2,700 internments over the period the cemetery was in use.

- By 1846 the records mention a proposed vault that *would not be for any particular congregation or persuasion, but for the <u>whole</u> town.*

- The care of the cemetery was the responsibility of the trustees of the Presbyterian Church. As the years advanced, there was a gradual deterioration of services. By 1849, many area residents had complained about the general neglect of the burying ground, and, in 1850, a letter of complaint appeared in a Georgetown newspaper, which caused grave concern to members of the Church. Steps were taken to clean up the cemetery and for the next 30 years they were successful.

- The first burial recorded in the Presbyterian Cemetery Records (Georgetown) was 25 August 1856 (54 years after the 1802 opening of the cemetery) when a child was buried. The record is rather a depressing metric of public health in the mid 1800s. The next two burials – just six days apart – were two more children from parish families.

- According to the records, the last internment was made in March of 1887.

As noted on previous pages, the Burial Ground succumbed to disrepair and eventually, in the early 20th Century, was purchased for a park by the DC Government. The Chapel was sold to other church congregations and eventually it fell into disrepair. The old chapel is now refurbished and is a private home.

Visitation Community Cemeteries

In 1799, three pious ladies settled into a small house adjacent to the then Georgetown College. Their spiritual guide was Father (later Archbishop) Leonard Neale. In 1816 they and their followers were formally professed as Sisters of the Visitation. Their Young Ladies Academy was later named the Georgetown Visitation Convent, which has become the Georgetown Visitation Preparatory School[xxx] while the community is now the Georgetown Visitation Monastery.

There are three burial places on the Visitation Monastery Campus:

1. A burial crypt under the chapel (1821 – 1841)
2. The Garden Cemetery (1841 – 1887)
3. The New Cemetery (1887 on)

The following Visitation campus map (Figure 21), from the Visitation web site, has been marked up with red figures to show the two cemeteries (Garden & New Cemeteries). The red oval with the number 2 next to it marks the Garden Cemetery while the red circle at the top of the picture (above the number 24) marks the New Cemetery. In addition, the Chapel with the 1821 – 1841 Crypt is numbered 3.

Figure 21 – Visitation Campus Map with Burial Areas Marked

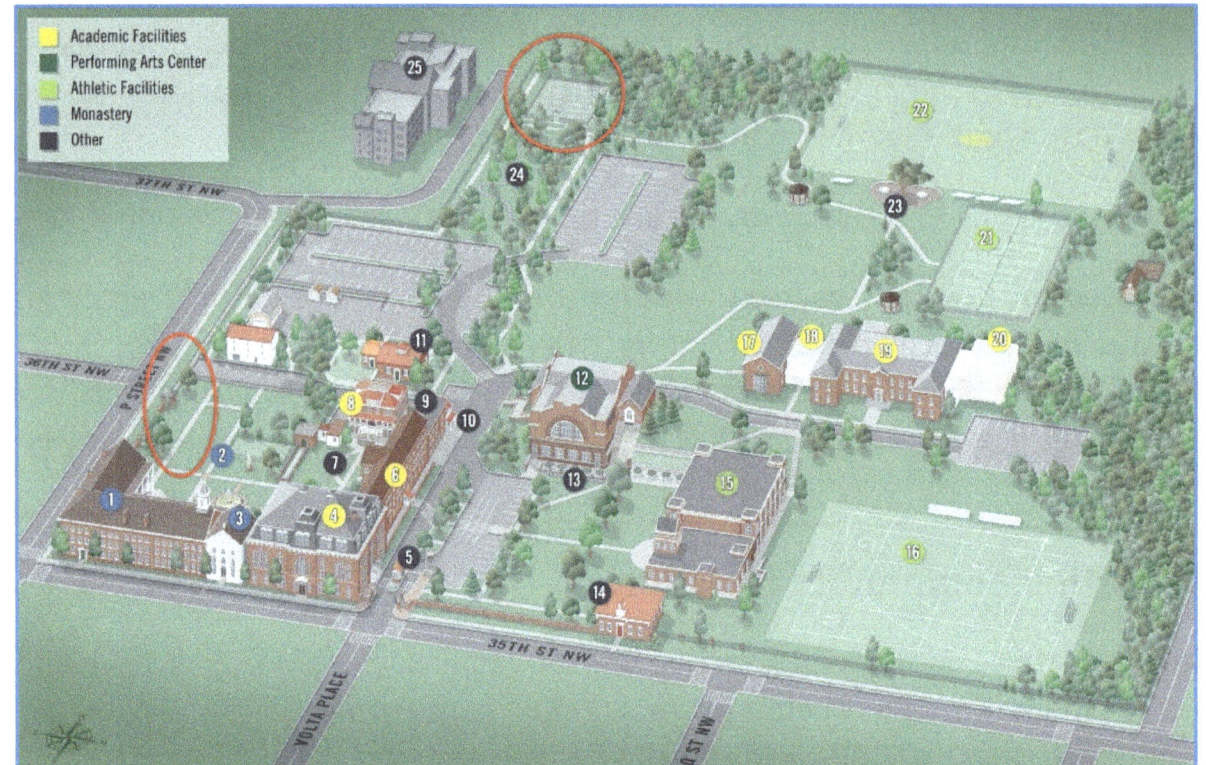

Visitation Burial Crypt

Below the Chapel of the Sacred Heart is a burial crypt as reported in the Department of the Interior's National Register of Historic Place Registration Form date stamped December 14, 1990.

> *Below the chapel is the brick vaulted crypt. There is one central tomb where the remains of Father Leonard Neale were re-interred after a renovation of the crypt in 1968. Father Cloriviere, 33 nuns and Father Robert Plunkett, first president of Georgetown College, are also buried in the crypt. The walls of the crypt are the exposed original brick but the floor is covered with highly polished peach colored marble installed in 1968.*[xxxi]

The items referenced in the figure: Neale's tomb, Cloriviére's sarcophagus, and Lalor's tombstone, can be seen predominantly in the picture of the Crypt found on page 56 in The Visitation – A monastic way of life in the Church. It is reproduced below as Figure 22.

Figure 22 – Visitation Crypt

- Crypt beneath the Chapel. Sarcophagus on pillars is Leonard Neale's tomb. Raised sarcophagus on floor is that of Father Cloriviére. Most important: tombstone visible to the left rear is that of Mother Teresa Lalor, foundress of this house.

In July 2019 John Kelly wrote a fascinating article in the Washington Post headlined: <u>Why is a French nobleman who tried to blow up Napoleon buried in Georgetown?</u> This amazing story is worth sharing here:

> *In the crypt below the chapel of the Georgetown Visitation Monastery at 35th and P streets NW is a flat marble slab inscribed with the story of the priest who is buried beneath it. Well, part of the story.*

The epitaph does not mention the priest's role in introducing to the world something that has become all too familiar: the improvised explosive device. Though the IED he helped create missed its intended target — Napoleon Bonaparte — it killed or wounded dozens of innocent bystanders.

This is the unlikely story of how Father Joseph Pierre Picot de Clorivière wound up at a convent where, to this day, he is revered as Visitation's "second founder."

Translated, the Latin on the tomb begins: "Here lies Joseph Pierre Picot de Clorivière. Born of a noble family of Brittany... The difficulties of the times and the will of Divine Providence forced him to leave his native land and to embark for this country, where he embraced the ecclesiastical vocation."

Divine Providence is notoriously difficult to intuit, but in 1800, Joseph Pierre Picot de Limoëlan — as he was then known — was certain it involved murdering Napoleon, who a year earlier had taken control of France in a coup. Limoëlan was not a priest then. He was a soldier from an aristocratic family. In the wake of the French Revolution, his family's lands had been confiscated and his father executed.

Limoëlan plotted with two co-conspirators — Robinault St. Réjant and François Carbon — to assassinate Napoleon. They chose to strike on the evening of Dec. 24, 1800, when they knew Napoleon would be riding in a carriage to the Paris premiere of Joseph Haydn's oratorio "The Creation."

The trio bought a horse and cart from a grain merchant and lashed a gunpowder-filled barrel to the cart. They positioned the vehicle along a street Napoleon would travel, Rue Saint-Nicaise. St. Réjant gave a girl a few coins to hold the horse in place while he stood at the back with a lighted pipe, awaiting a signal from Limoëlan to light the fuse.

Either because Napoleon's carriage was moving too quickly or the gunpowder was of poor quality, the blast came too late to claim its intended victim. But it claimed plenty of others.

As a historian later wrote: "Mangled and distorted corpses were lying in heaps on the muddy pavements; shrieks of pain and anguish were heard in almost every house; bewildered persons ran aimlessly in every direction."

The episode — the first of many unsuccessful attempts to eliminate Napoleon — became known as the Plot of the Infernal Machine.

"The infernal machine was a 17th-century barrel bomb used in sieges," wrote Jonathan North, the author of "Killing Napoleon: The Plot to Blow Up Bonaparte," in an email to Answer Man. "This time the plotters deployed it in the streets of Paris."

Wrote North: "People were shocked that the plotters had added metal fragments to the barrel and placed paving stones around it to increase the number of fragments thrown into the street. Another shocking element was that it had all taken place on Christmas Eve when the streets were packed."

Nine people were killed outright, including the girl the plotters had hired to hold the reins. All that was left of her was her feet.

French authorities raced to solve the crime. Although the horse and cart had been obliterated, they pieced together the remnants as best they could and invited the public to view them. The grain dealer recognized the horse as one he had recently sold.

St. Réjant and Carbon were picked up, tried and sent to the guillotine. Limoëlan managed to evade capture.

In 1805, Limoëlan made his way to the United States. He earned money as a painter of miniature portraits. (Two are in the collection of New York's Metropolitan Museum of Art.) He later entered a Maryland seminary to train as a priest. He took his vows in 1812, shedding the name Limoëlan and refashioning himself as Father Clorivière. (An uncle of the same name was a prominent Jesuit.)

Clorivière first served a parish in Charleston, S.C., then in 1819 was sent to lead the convent in Georgetown.

Clorivière quickly embarked on an ambitious improvement program, designing a new chapel and other buildings himself. He largely paid for them himself, too, donating his French military pension and the proceeds of land in France he had sold to his brother-in-law. He taught the sisters French and improved the quality of the curriculum they offered at their parochial school, said Sister Mada-anne Gell, archivist of the Georgetown Visitation Monastery Archives.

Forgiveness and absolution are central tenets of Catholicism. So is penance. Sister Mada-anne feels Clorivière must have undergone a "conversion of heart," a realization he had sinned and a determination to repair the damage.

After Clorivière's death in 1826, the nuns followed his instructions and burned his diaries. What did they know of his past? They surely must have wondered why the French priest spent every Christmas Eve in the chapel, weeping.

Visitation Community Cemetery (The Garden Cemetery)

In 1841 the Georgetown Visitation Monastery established the Visitation Community Cemetery now known as the "Garden Cemetery". That cemetery was used until 1887 when the New Cemetery was opened in the southwest corner of the 22-acre Visitation campus. The Garden Cemetery has 78 graves from 1841 to 1887 – these are all for sisters who were members of the Visitation Monastery.[xxxii] While the National Register of Historic places uses 1887 as the date of the New Cemetery, The Visitation – A monastic way of life in the Church uses 1880, on page 57.

The following Library of Congress picture (Figure 23) from 1890 shows the Garden Cemetery. The picture reflects the simplicity with which the members of the Monastery lived and died.

Figure 23 – Visitation Garden Cemetery in 1890

Visitation New Cemetery

The new cemetery was opened in the late 1880s adjacent to the Georgetown University campus, close to where Holy Trinity's Cemetery #2 was located. The cemetery can be seen through the fence, which is across from walkway to the east of the Reiss Science Center, as seen in Figure 24.

Figure 24 – Visitation New Cemetery in 2020

Each tombstone lists the following information about the deceased member of the Visitation Order: Name, date of death, age at death, number of years since they professed faith to the Order, and R. I. P., which is the abbreviation for the Latin expression *Requiescat in Pace – May She Rest in Peace*. Figure 25 shows the details of a typical tombstone.

Figure 25 – Details of a Tombstone - Visitation New Cemetery

The following picture (Figure 26) is of the entrance to New Cemetery taken in 2015. The entrance sign says, I AM THE RESURRECTION AND THE LIFE.

Figure 26 – Entrance to the Visitation New Cemetery

Figure 7 shows both the Visitation New Cemetery as well as the site of the second Holy Trinity Cemetery – located on the Georgetown Campus.

Yarrow Mamout Private Burial Site

Of all the private burial sites (typically family plots), one stands out from several aspects – Mamout was very distinct from the majority of land owners in Georgetown in the early 1800s. Mamout was taken by slave traders from Africa at the age of 16 and was literate in Arabic and a practicing Muslim his whole life. After being granted his freedom he bought property in Georgetown and after two financial failures became a very rich man. He remained a faithful Muslim all his life and was buried in a corner of the property, now identified as 3324 Dent Place NW.

His remarkable life and the recent archeological dig on his former property led me to include him in this book. He and his family have been written about before. James H. Johnson's book From Slave Ship to Harvard: Yarrow Mamout and the History of an African American Family tells the remarkable trajectory of this family. I have copied the following review on Johnson's book from the Amazon web site.

> *From Slave Ship to Harvard is the true story of an African American family in Maryland over six generations. The author has reconstructed a unique narrative of black struggle and achievement from paintings, photographs, books, diaries, court records, legal documents, and oral histories. From Slave Ship to Harvard traces the family from the colonial period and the American Revolution through the Civil War to Harvard and finally today.*
>
> *Yarrow Mamout, the first of the family in America, was an educated Muslim from Guinea. He was brought to Maryland on the slave ship Elijah and gained his freedom forty-four years later. By then, Yarrow had become so well known in the Georgetown section of Washington, D.C., that he attracted the attention of the eminent American portrait painter Charles Willson Peale, who captured Yarrow's visage in the painting that appears on the cover of this book. The author here reveals that Yarrow's immediate relatives—his sister, niece, wife, and*

son—were notable in their own right. His son married into the neighboring Turner family, and the farm community in western Maryland called Yarrowsburg was named for Yarrow Mamout's daughter-in-law, Mary "Polly" Turner Yarrow. The Turner line ultimately produced Robert Turner Ford, who graduated from Harvard University in 1927.

Just as Peale painted the portrait of Yarrow, James H. Johnston's new book puts a face on slavery and paints the history of race in Maryland. It is a different picture from what most of us imagine. Relationships between blacks and whites were far more complex, and the races more dependent on each other. Fortunately, as this one family's experience shows, individuals of both races repeatedly stepped forward to lessen divisions and to move America toward the diverse society of today.[xxxiii]

In the summer of 2015, there was an archeological dig at the Georgetown site in an attempt to verify the story as written by the painter Charles Wilson Peale in an obituary for Mamout who died in 1823, allegedly at 138 years of age. It was later determined that he was 83 years old when he died and had exaggerated his age! Not surprisingly, there are still different estimates of his actual age when he died. Peale had earlier painted Mamout's picture (1819) and it hangs in the Atwater Museum in Philadelphia. A photo of it is shown in Figure 27.

Later, in 1822, another portrait of Mamout was done by then 17-year-old James Alexander Simpson.[xxxiv] Simpson is listed by the Smithsonian as part time teacher of painting at Georgetown College. The 1822 portrait hangs in the Georgetown Public Library.

Figure 27 – Peale's 1819 Portrait of Yarrow Mamout

While the dig failed to locate the foundation of the original house or a burial spot it was considered a success by those who organized it. They have published a report on the Worldwide Web: *The Yarrow Mamout Archaeology*

Buried in Georgetown

Project unearths the history of a prominent 1800s African Muslim[xxxv]; January 26, 2016. It is summarized below.

> *Yarrow Mamout was an African Muslim born in Guinea, West Africa in 1736, where he was thought to have been a member of the nomadic Fulani tribe. He was sold into slavery at the age of 16 and was brought to Maryland. After 44 years of being a "good and faithful servant," he was rewarded with his freedom.*
>
> *Mamout was able to read and write in Arabic, and was known to have an "extensive understanding" of real estate, finance, and law. He exhibited his business acumen when he purchased shares at the Bank of Georgetown and was able to live comfortably off of the interest for the rest of his long, long life.*
>
> *Mamout purchased property in Georgetown at 3324 Dent Place in 1800, just four years after receiving his freedom. It was rumored that he was also buried on this property after he died in 1823, at 87 years old.*
>
> *In 2012, the City Archaeologist in Washington D.C., Dr. Ruth Trocolli, was informed by researcher James Johnston that the privately-owned property, and potential burial site of Yarrow Mamout, was at risk of being disturbed. The District wanted to demolish the neglected 1850s house that stood on the property that had been partially destroyed by Hurricane Irene in 2011, and potential developers wanted to split the parcel of land into two lots.*
>
> *University of Florida Department of Anthropology Ph.D. student and National Science Foundation Graduate Research Fellow Mia L. Carey, M.A., led this archaeological dig in the heart of Washington, D.C., searching for evidence of Mamout's life and remains. This dig was significant for a number of reasons.*
>
> *"There has never been an archaeological site excavated where the Muslim identity of the individual was confirmed in the home or property," Carey explains. "No other site like this exists in America."*

African Muslims were unique in the enslaved population in America because they were literate, well-spoken, and well-traveled – "cosmopolitan in a sense," as Carey describes. Roughly fifteen to forty percent of the American slave population was Muslim; however, many lost their Islam identities as a result of being in a hostile Christian environment.

Mamout was able to maintain his devotion to Islam until his death in 1823, and was also an important figure during his time. He sat for two formal portraits – an exceedingly rare thing for an African to have done in the 18th and 19th centuries. The first was painted in 1819 by Charles Wilson Peale, who also painted portraits of American Revolutionary icons like Thomas Jefferson, Benjamin Franklin, and George Washington (whom Mamout is said to have met). That portrait now hangs in the Atwater Museum in Philadelphia.

The second portrait, painted in 1822 by James Alexander Simpson, is displayed in the Peabody Room of the Georgetown Public Library, where it caught the attention of D.C.-based lawyer, writer, and lecturer <u>James H. Johnston</u>, who wondered who this mystery African man was to have sat for a formal portrait that would then hang in such an institution.

Johnston went on to write the book <u>From Slave Ship to Harvard: Yarrow Mamout and the History of an African American Family</u>, documenting six generations of the African American family that began with Mamout. After seven years of research and writing, the book was published, igniting local interest in Mamout's story as an important piece of local history. The popularity of Mamout's story led to Carey and her team having the opportunity to excavate the property that was once his home.

…

Carey enjoys telling Mamout's story, and the story of his fellow African Muslims who were brought to America against their will and who had a profound impact on the cultural and intellectual legacy of this country, an impact almost unknown today for being largely invisible and unacknowledged.

...

This research, she says, opened her own eyes to how diverse the Muslim population really is. Even more so, it opened her eyes to the long history of Muslims in America, and inspired her to change the focus of her dissertation.

"It changed my perspective," she says. "My dissertation is now focused on how public archaeology can be used to inform the public on the understudied African Muslim presence in America. ..."

The dig was completed in November 2015. Unfortunately, they did not find the foundation of Mamout's original home or his burial site, though Carey continues to analyze artifacts in her lab in Florida in the hopes of finding something definitively related to him. But, regardless of the results of the dig, for Carey it was still a success.

"I went to graduate school with the purpose of giving voice to the voiceless, telling the stories you might not be taught in history classes," she says. "... but I was so intrigued by having the opportunity to tell Mamout's story, and that is what made me want to get involved and learn more." Figure 28 below, shows Carey, her students and possibly others at the dig site.[xxxvi]

Figure 28 – Photograph of Yarrow Mamout Archaeological Dig

Bibliography

Fletcher, Carlton, *Burial Grounds of Holy Trinity Church, Georgetown, D.C.*, Newsletter of the Catholic Historical Society of Washington, Volume X, Number 3, July-September, 2002.

Heritage Committee, Georgetown Presbyterian Church. *The Presbyterian Congregation In George Town 1780 – 1970*. Published by the Session of The Presbyterian Congregation in George Town. Washington, DC 1971. (Jolene Blozis, Chair, Heritage Committee, Georgetown Presbyterian Church graciously provided me with a copy of this booklet in response to a question I asked in 2016.)

Jackson, Richard P. *The Chronicles of Georgetown, D.C. From 1751 To 1878*. Washington, DC: R. O. Polkinhorn, Printer.

Lesko, Kathleen Menzie, Babb, Valerie M., and Gibbs, Carroll R. *Black Georgetown Remembered*. ISBN 978-1-64712-165-5. Published by Georgetown University Press, Washington, DC.

Sluby, Paul E. Sr. Washington, DC 1975. *The Old Methodist Burying Ground*. Published by the Mt. Zion Cemetery Commission. Washington, DC.

Sluby, Paul E. SR. *Bury Me Deep – Burial Places Past and Present In and Nearby Washington, D.C.* ISBN 978-1-61584-107-3. A Self-Published Historical Review and Reference Manual 2009.

Sluby, Paul; E. SR. and Wormley, Stanton L. *Presbyterian Cemetery Records (Georgetown) Washington, DC 1956-1897*. Online Computer Library Center number: OCLC22570642. Published by The Columbian Harmony Society. Washington, DC 1990.

Peter T. Higgins

Stanley, Karol L. *History of Georgetown Lutheran Church 1769 -(250)- 2019*. Published by Select Printing & Copying, Washington, DC 2019.

The Visitation – A monastic way of life in the Church. ISBN 978-2-7468-2091-3. Published by Éditions du Signe. Strasbourg, Cedex 2, France.

Researchers of Note

Fletcher, Carlton

Fletcher received his degrees from the Rhode Island School of Design (BFA, 1972), and American University (MFA, 1982), and was one of the founding members of the Washington Studio School (1985). He is an historian of Glover Park, Washington, DC. The Web Site Glover Park History has a section Historical Sketches of Glover Park, Upper Georgetown, and Georgetown Heights by Carlton Fletcher. He has well documented references for his historical descriptions.

Jackson, Richard P.

Jackson, a Native of Georgetown and Member of the Washington Bar. In 1878 Jackson wrote The Chronicles of Georgetown, D.C. from 1751 to 1878. His Preface to the Chronicles starts out: *To compile this book, during my leisure hours, has been more a labor of love than an expectation of gain; to snatch from oblivion what otherwise would be lost, and to refresh the memories of our citizens of the facts and events that have transpired in a lifetime, and leave to the rising generation a history of the town (though imperfect) to which reference can be made to learn how our ancestors struggled amidst adversity to build a city, with churches and institutions of learning, that should be a credit to themselves and a benefit to posterity.*

Lesko, Kathleen Menzie

Lesko, along with Valerie M. Babb and Carroll R. Gibbs, researched and edited the 30th Anniversary Edition of <u>Black Georgetown Remembered</u>. They also produced a documentary video Black Georgetown Remembered, which can be found online and at the Special Collections Room of Georgetown University's Lauinger Library. It has over 50 interviews as well as numerous pictures of interest.

Sluby, Paul E. Sluby, SR.

Sluby was a prolific researcher and author of <u>Bury Me Deep – Burial Places Past and Present in and Nearby Washington, D.C.</u> and co-author of <u>Presbyterian Cemetery records (Georgetown) Washington, DC 1956-1897</u> with Stanton L. Wormley. (In 2015 I came across Sluby's marvelous research document, <u>Bury Me Deep - Burial Places Past and Present in and nearby Washington, DC – A Historical Review and Reference Manual</u> by Paul E. Sluby, Sr. The book was no longer available in print by 2015. Paul and I talked briefly and he sold me a digital copy of his book on a CD. Mr. Sluby refers to cemeteries as *marble orchards*, putting a nice phrase on sometimes sad places. His research skills were likely enhanced based on his training and professional experiences as a Detective in the Washington, DC Metropolitan Police Department. I learned in late 2021 that Mr. Sluby died March 27, 2019. He is buried at the National Harmony Memorial Park in Landover, MD.

Wormley, Stanton L.

Wormley attended Howard University and received his Ph.D. from Cornell University in 1939. He co-authored <u>Presbyterian Cemetery records (Georgetown) Washington, DC 1956-1897</u> with Paul E. Sluby, SR. Dr. Stanton taught at Virginia State College from 1932 to 1938 and Howard University from 1938 to 1971.[xxxvii]

Acknowledgments

- In researching and writing this book, my son, KC Higgins, an avid researcher, author of house histories, and coauthor of a book on Cleveland Park, was extremely helpful. KC provided much needed editing services.

- I have found the resources of the Historic American Building Survey (HABS) to be very useful in gaining details from the applications for being considered for a HABS project as are the final work products.

- Likewise, I have found the resources of the Historic American Landscape Survey (HALS) to be very useful in gaining details from the applications for being considered for a HALS project as are the final work products.

- The DC Library's Georgetown Branch's Peabody Room, so well managed by Jerry McCoy, has always been an important stop in any research into the history of the Georgetown area.

- The research of Carlton Fletcher has proved to be invaluable. Fletcher is the researcher and writer at www.gloverparkhistory.com.

- There are several websites that were helpful in finding historical facts and leads to other sources, among them:

- I have found the resources of the District of Columbia Library's Special Collections (particularly its online newspaper archives) to be critical in many research tasks.

- Several Church and Cemetery web sites.

- The Findagrave.com web site

- The StreetsofWashington.com web site

- Wikipedia – when the articles have solid references to other sources.

Appendix A: Orientation to Georgetown of 1796

This 1796 map shows the old street names in Georgetown before the City of Washington integrated Georgetown into the lager city street grid in 1895. The two anchors to the Figure 29 map and to Georgetown itself are **High Street** and **Falls Street / Bridge Street**.

Figure 29 – 1796 Map of Georgetown

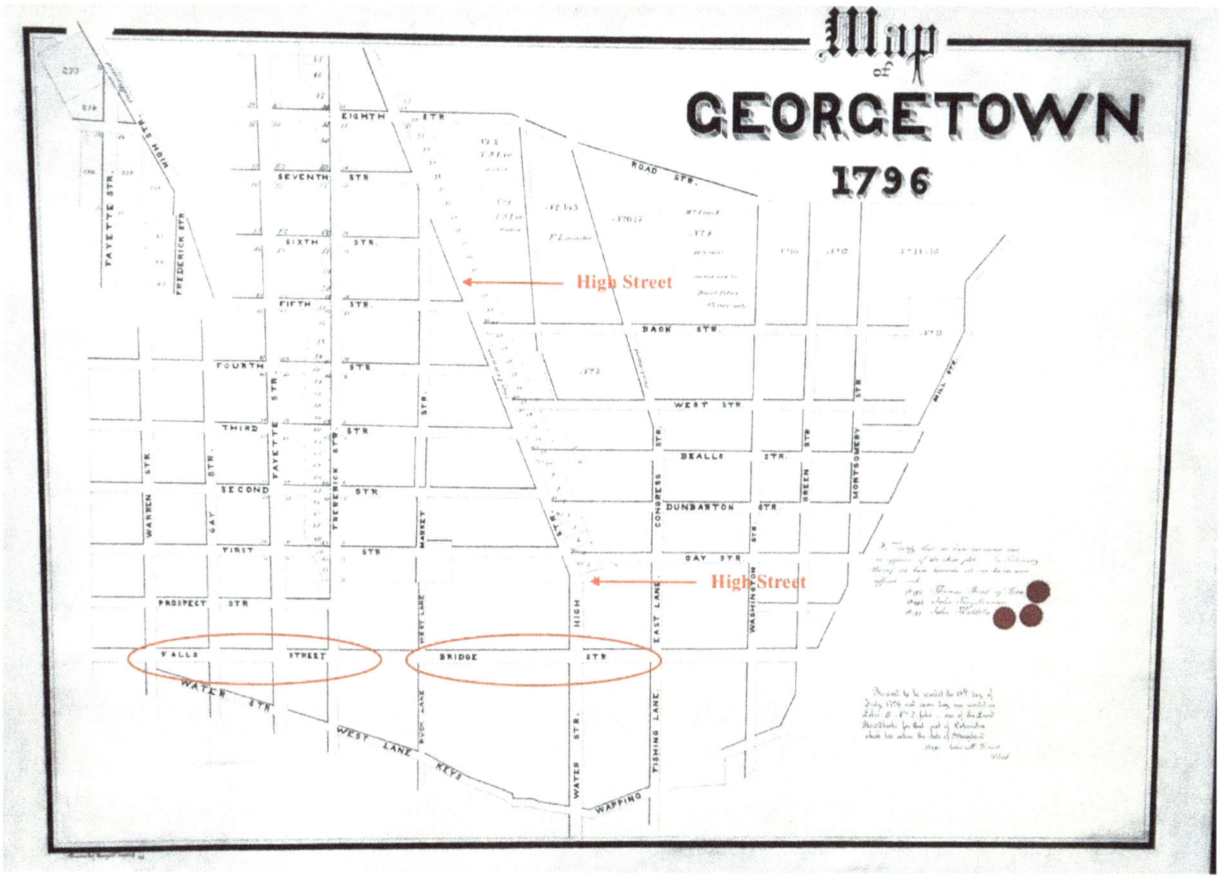

The name High Street is used in the United Kingdom and many parts of the Commonwealth for the main shopping street. Georgetown's High Street eventually was renamed Wisconsin Avenue, which, over time became a main shopping street. Interestingly in the 1800s the main shopping street in Georgetown was aptly named Market Street and it is now known as 33rd Street.

In an unusual arrangement, today's Wisconsin Ave had two different names depending on which side of modern-day M Street you were on. Above M Street it was known as High Street all the way to at least the upper end of Georgetown while between M Street and the river it was known as Water Street. It remained High Street until 1895.[xxxviii]

Today's M Street was also known by two different names. Between Foggy Bottom and today's 33rd Street it was called Bridge Street while west of 33rd Street it was called Falls Street.

Bridge Street was named for the bridge over Rock Creek. The web site, Streets of Washington, explains:

> *Many people know about the old Aqueduct Bridge that preceded the Key Bridge over the Potomac and that we profiled previously. But there's another Georgetown bridge that still carries both water and traffic safely across a separate body of water, thus serving as a functioning aqueduct. The bridge in question is the one carrying Pennsylvania Avenue over Rock Creek and the Rock Creek & Potomac Parkway at the eastern edge of Georgetown.*
>
> *For the first half of the 19th century, Pennsylvania Avenue's western terminus was at Rock Creek. If you wanted to continue over the creek to Georgetown you had to go north and take the rickety wooden M Street bridge, the historic crossing that had given the eastern stretch of M Street in Georgetown the name Bridge Street.*[xxxix]

Falls Street refers to the road that led from Georgetown to the Little Falls of the Potomac River, where a toll bridge was built. The Chronicles of Georgetown, D.C. from 1751 to 1878[xl] provides the details of this interesting bridge, which has been replaced several times due to floods and ice flows. The details from The Chronicles are summarized below:

Buried in Georgetown

Falls Bridge is located at the Little Falls of the Potomac River, three miles above town.

The Legislature of Maryland, by an act of 1791, incorporated the Georgetown Bridge Company, for the purpose of erecting a toll bridge at the Little Falls of the Potomac River. Afterwards, upon the destruction of the bridge in February, 1811, Congress authorized the company to make a new assessment upon its stockholders to rebuild the bridge and keep the same in repair, together with the road leading thereto from Georgetown.

This bridge, built of timber, was supported by immense cable chains stretching from pier to pier, from which the term "Chain Bridge," is derived. ...

The building of the Chesapeake and Ohio Canal in Georgetown, starting in 1828, closed several formerly through streets. As a result, some road bridges were built over the canal to the east of High Street / Water Street while some pedestrian bridges were built to the west.

The word Columbia always intrigued me. Was it a play on Columbus? Several years ago, I learned that the names of countries and some other things could be expressed in Latin by adding *"ia"* to the end. Thus, Britain becomes Britannia and Columbus becomes Columbia, etc.

Appendix B: A Brief History of Georgetown 1632 – 1899

Georgetown, the early days

In 1632 King Charles I granted George Calvert, 1st Baron Baltimore, a charter to found a colony east of the Potomac River. That same year, George Calvert died, and the charter was given to his son, Cecil Calvert, who became the 2nd Baron Baltimore. The first settlers of the Maryland Colony included a mix of about 200 Catholics and Protestants who had been promised land grants. They arrived on the ships the <u>Ark</u> and the <u>Dove</u> and established the English Colony of Maryland.[xli]

That same year, English fur trader Henry Fleet first documented a Native American (the Nacotchtank tribe) village called Tahoga on the site of present-day Georgetown and established trade there.[xlii] Interestingly, about 350 years later a Tahoga Restaurant, which one reviewer stated *was named after the Indian tribe that once inhabited the land where Georgetown sits*, opened at 2815 M Street. The reviewer had the right idea but confused the village name (Tahoga) with the tribal name (Nacotchtank). The Tahoga Restaurant was enjoyed by many, including the author, for several years before closing.

1740s

In approximately 1745 George Gordon constructed a tobacco inspection house along the Potomac in what is now Georgetown. Tobacco was already being transferred from land to waterways at this location, when the inspection house was built. Warehouses, wharves, and other buildings were then constructed around the inspection house, and it quickly became a small community. It did not take long before Georgetown grew into a thriving port, facilitating trade and shipments of tobacco and other goods from colonial Virginia and Maryland to England. Situated on the fall line, Georgetown was the farthest point upstream to which oceangoing boats could navigate the Potomac River.[xliii]

1750s

In 1751 Georgetown was incorporated as a town and first regularly settled, when the area was still part of the British colony of the Province of Maryland. Georgetown was located on land that was owned by George Gordon and George Beall. The Maryland Legislature purchased 60 acres of land for the town from Gordon and Beall at the price of £280 and the town was named George Town after King George II of England.[xliv]

1760s

In 1765 the longest surviving, private home in Washington, DC, was built and has been basically unchanged other than additions (e.g., a second floor) in the 1800s; it is now a national historic site in Georgetown, named the Old Stone House. It is located in the 3040 block of M Street.

In 1766 Col. John Beatty established the Georgetown Lutheran Church, at the corner of High and Fourth Streets (now known as the corner of Wisconsin Ave. and Volta Place). Their first building, a log cabin, was erected in 1769. The church building fell into disrepair and faced a reclaim of the land by the donor.

1770s

Significant expansion of the acreage of Georgetown started in 1770. Carlton Fletcher describes the major additions:[xlv]

> *When Georgetown was founded in 1752, it only had 80 lots, or about sixty acres, but, starting in 1770, additions were annexed to the city, and increased it tenfold. Additions were land tracts carved by their owners into lots, blocks and streets, and the first of these was when Charles Beatty and George Fraser Hawkins used their 1745 purchase to create Beatty and Hawkins Addition to Georgetown--"304 lots as parcels of ground, divided by proper streets and lanes, for the enlargement of George Town and the general publick (sic) benefit" -- recorded at Frederick, Maryland, on May 17, 1770. The next month three hundred lots were sold by lottery--the ticket-buyer only found out afterwards which lot he had acquired.*
>
> *In 1753, James Hopkins, brother and heir-at-law of the late Matthew Hopkins, sold Henry Threlkeld three tracts of land, totaling 629 acres, for 100 pounds.*

In today's world it would be unthinkable to buy a building lot or a house via lottery and after paying you ended up owning a random lot or house.

1780s

In 1782 a group of Scottish worshipers built the Presbyterian Church of Georgetown, which eventually has a burial ground adjacent to the church. They had been meeting in homes since 1760.

By 1789 the Jesuits established Georgetown University on the west end of Georgetown – originally the school was established as Georgetown College. The first graduating class was in 1794.

In 1789 the Maryland State Legislature formally issued the George Town charter, which incorporated the town. It had been initially established in 1751 when it was a still in a British colony.

Georgetown in the early days of The District Of Columbia

1790s

The 1790 The Residence Act created the District of Columbia and authorized President Washington to select the location – along the Potomac River.

The following quote outlines the creation of the District quite nicely.[xlvi]

> *After the US Constitution (1787) provided that a tract of land be reserved for the seat of the federal government, both Maryland and Virginia offered parcels for that purpose; on 16 July 1790, Congress authorized George Washington to choose a site not more than 10 mi (16 km) square along the Potomac River. President Washington made his selection in January 1791.*

By 1791 the City of Washington was established. While Washington was still alive, he referred to it as *The Federal City*.[xlvii] The Forrest-Marbury House, at 3350 M Street (formerly Falls Street), is where George Washington met with local landowners on March 29, 1791 to acquire the land for the District of Columbia. Later when Marbury owned the house – the Supreme Court ruled in the Marbury VS. Madison case, establishing the right of judicial review of congressional action.

Figure 30 – Forest Marbury House History Plaque

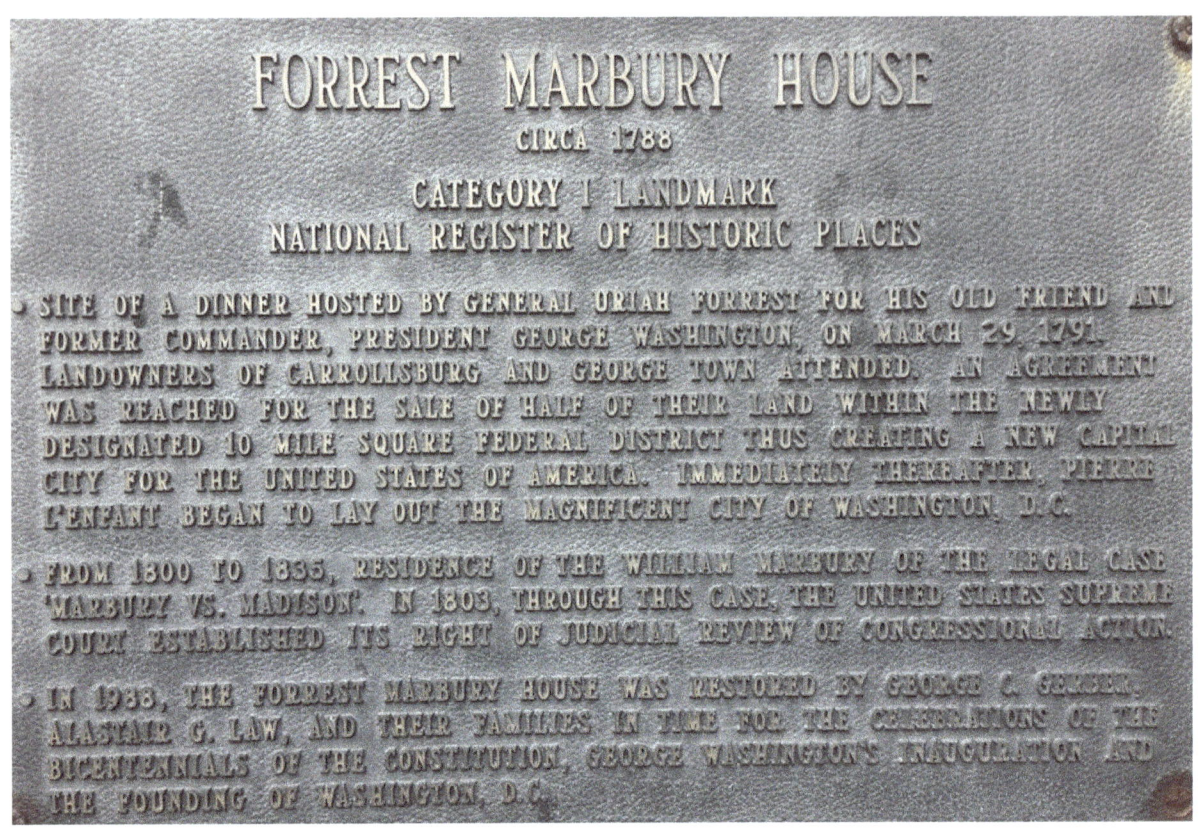

That same year John Threlkeld concluded the purchase of several land grants that were larger than the existing Town of Georgetown at that point in time. These land grants, had been consolidated by John Threlkeld into a tract named *Alliance*, whose extent can be judged by the fact that it included what is now Georgetown University, Foxhall Village, Burleith, Hillandale, Wesley Heights, Whitehaven Park, Glover-Archbold Park, and much of Glover Park.[xlviii]

In 1792 the Jesuits of Georgetown College established the Holy Trinity Catholic Church in Georgetown. The original church building, opened in 1794, still exists at 3513 N Street and is used for daily masses. The church later established what is the third documented cemetery in Georgetown – originally a Graveyard adjacent to the church.

1800s

In 1802 the Bridge Street Presbyterian Church established a graveyard next to the Meeting House - the second documented cemetery in Georgetown.

In 1808 the Jesuit community of Georgetown University established a Jesuit Community Cemetery as a final resting place for members of their community – on the College campus. Over time it was relocated to its present location on the campus.

In 1808 the Dumbarton Street Methodist Episcopal Church purchased the land for what became known as the Old Methodist Episcopal Burying Ground. At that point the membership of the Dumbarton Street M.E. Church was fifty percent Black, consisting of both free Blacks and enslaved Blacks. While Georgetown itself was about thirty percent Black.

1810s

On October 16, 1816 the Black members of the Dumbarton Street M.E. Church formed the Mount Zion Methodist Church. This was the first Black Methodist Church in Washington, DC according to a historic plaque on the church building. This church, at 1334 29th St., is the oldest known church in DC started by and for Black people, and was part of Underground Railway.[xlix] Eventually Mt. Zion Methodist Church had a cemetery that is described in the alphabetical listing of cemeteries.

In 1817 the Georgetown Visitation Monastery established a cemetery for members of that community.

In 1817 Holy Trinity moved the remains in their church graveyard to land on the College campus. This new location was later called the Second Holy Trinity Cemetery. They continued to use both locations after 1817.

1820s

In 1820, the Georgetown Presbyterian Bridge Street moved the remains in their church graveyard to the Presbyterian Burial Ground at the block defined by today's 33rd Street, 34th Street, Q Street, and Volta Place.

1830s

In 1832 Holy Trinity Church purchased land in Beatty & Hawkins' Extension of Georgetown, in what is now Glover Park, for an expansion of their cemetery capacity.

In 1834 Georgetown experienced a major outbreak of a cholera epidemic, which kept the cemeteries busy.

1840s

In 1849 the US Congress chartered the Oak Hill Cemetery on R Street, east of Wisconsin Ave, (R Street was known as Road Street at that time).

In 1849 Holy Trinity closed their Graveyard on the church grounds as they were planning on using the land to build a new and larger church building. They moved the remains in their church graveyard to the Second Holy Trinity Cemetery, on the College campus.

1850s

In 1850 the Oak Hill Cemetery Chapel, designed by James Renwick, JR. was built.

In 1850 slave auctions were outlawed in the City of Washington including Georgetown.

On the 1851 Map of Georgetown, used in this book, we note that in 1851 the Georgetown population was 8,366 people.

In 1855 the District of Columbia started maintaining a Register of Deaths. During the Civil War the Register was not maintained. By 1871 Certificates of Death were being issued as well as entering the deaths in the Register of Deaths.

Georgetown – Emancipation And the Civil War

1860s

On April 16, 1862 Congress abolished slavery in the District of Columbia (including Georgetown) nine months before Lincoln's Emancipation

Proclamation of January 1, 1863.^l This legislation in 1862 freed nearly 3,200 Washingtonians, while paying their enslavers for their release.^li After the Civil War many African Americans moved to Georgetown establishing a thriving Black community.^lii

October 5, 1862 the First Baptist Church was established in Georgetown at 2624 Dumbarton Street. The church building was rebuilt in September 1882.^liii

1870s

In 1871 Georgetown lost its charter and merged with the city and county of Washington. This marked the end of independent municipalities in DC. Up until then, since the formation of the District of Columbia (December 1, 1800), Georgetown had remained an independent city within the new capital.

In 1871 the District of Columbia started issuing Death Certificates.

In 1878, Congress revoked the District's limited democracy and imposed an appointed commissioner system that lasted until 1967. In doing so, Congress redubbed Georgetown as "West Washington".^liv The name was used sparingly and eventually fell into disuse.

In 1879 the Mount Zion Methodist Church took over the Old Methodist Episcopal Burying Ground and the Female Union Band Society Graveyard, which over time have become known as the Mount Zion Cemetery. The Mt Zion Cemetery is located at 27th street just north of Q Street.

Georgetown – at the end of the 19th Century

1890s

Rock Creek Park was authorized by Congress in 1890 to preserve a relatively undeveloped area of farms and woodlands to serve as *"a public park and pleasuring ground"* for the nation's capital.

The development of the park road system saw significant changes to the land around the already closed down Lyon's Great Mill.

> *Just north of Georgetown stood this large merchant mill equipped with two water wheels, one on each end of the sturdy structure. The two-story mill was made of brick and had a basement level of native blue stone. It probably did more business than any of the other mills along Rock Creek. It was built in 1780 on the east side of the creek just across from the eastern boundary of Oak Hill Cemetery. Lyons Mill Road used to connect it with Georgetown via a bridge over the creek and a road that ran up the hill on the west side of the creek. The bridge's abutments are now used for a pedestrian bridge over the creek. The mill was part of a 65-acre estate that included a barn, smokehouse, icehouse, carriage house, stable, and two stone houses. The half-mile long mill race, the longest of any on Rock Creek, powered the mill's two massive water wheels. The mill ground its last flour in 1875, when its last owner died. By the early 1880s it briefly became popular as a rendezvous for "barn dances, picnics, masquerades, and other fashionable functions," but later was abandoned and fell into decay. The remaining structure collapsed in 1913.* [lv]

Over the years the street names in Georgetown have changed significantly – in part to align them with the names of streets in the rest of the city, where appropriate. Figure 31 below, shows the street names in 1899 as well as the two canals that ended in Georgetown. Sections of the canal that crossed the Potomac, on an Aqueduct, then continued down to Alexandria. They can still be seen today along some of the roads from Key Bridge towards Alexandria.

While the Figure 31 map shows the core area of Georgetown it does not show all of the additions made over time. It does show (highlighted with a red oval) Lyons Mill Road on the upper right-hand side of the street grid. Three of our cemeteries are located adjacent to Lyons Mill Road. Today this roadbed is washed out but it serves as a footpath down from 27th Street to Rock Creek Park. The map does not have the cemetery names on it, thus the following guide is provided to assist the reader:

1. Oak Hill Cemetery is to the left of Lyons Mill Road, in an area with the pink stripes

2. Mount Zion Cemetery, which is composed of two separate adjacent cemeteries, in an area to the right of Lyons Mill Road with a non-striped background.

Figure 31 – 1899 Map of Georgetown

with Lyons Mill Road Marked

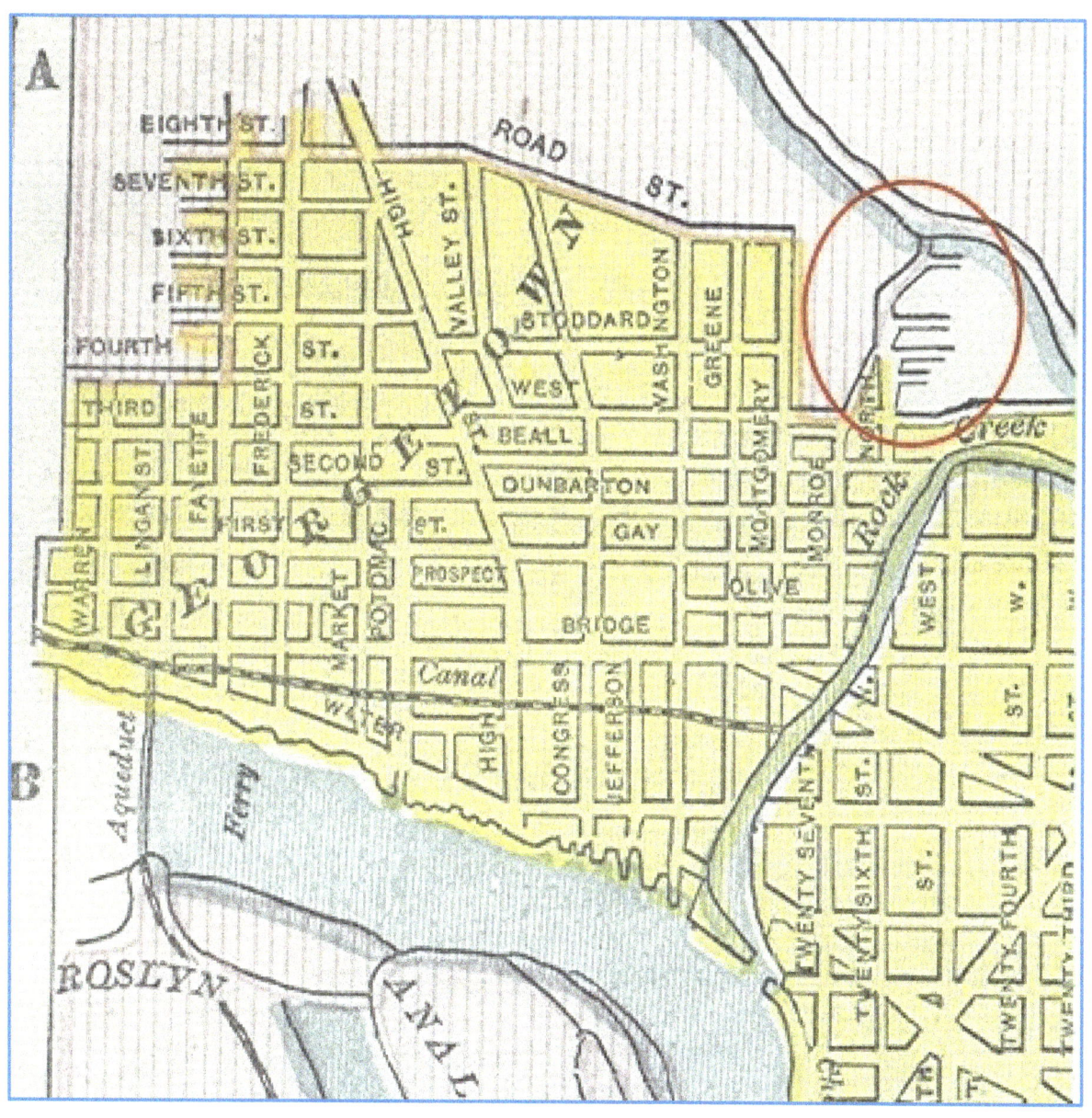

End Notes

[i] From the historic plaque on the Mt. Zion United Methodist Church

[ii] The Aged Woman's Home of Georgetown web site: https://agedwomanshome.org/history/

[iii] HABS No. DC-105 (Page 3)

[iv] https://georgetownlutheran.com/history/

[v] History of Georgetown Lutheran Church 1769 (250) 2019, A history of the community by Karol L. Stanley

[vi] https://www.glc250.org/history-notes-blog/archives/10-2019

[vii] From the web: http://www.library.georgetown.edu/infrequently-asked-questions/it-true-jesuit-community-cemetery-was-originally-different-location-cam

[viii] https://www.findagrave.com/cemetery/2433996/holy-trinity-cemetery-%25232

[ix] BURY ME DEEP, Burial Places Past and Present in and Nearby Washington, D.C. A Historical Review and Reference Manual by Paul S. Sluby, Sr., Page 93

[x] Burial Grounds of Holy Trinity Church, Georgetown, D.C., Carlton Fletcher, Newsletter of the Catholic Historical Society of Washington, Volume X, Number 3, July-September, 2002

[xi] https://www.findagrave.com/cemetery/2433996/holy-trinity-cemetery-%25232

[xii] Burial Grounds of Holy Trinity Church, Georgetown, D.C., Carlton Fletcher, Newsletter of the Catholic Historical Society of Washington, Volume X, Number 3, July-September, 2002

xiii https://gloverparkhistory.com/geography/streets/old-streets-of-upper-georgetown/

xiv http://www.streetsofwashington.com/2013/08/on-pennsylvania-ave-georgetowns-other.html

xv

https://memory.loc.gov/master/pnp/habshaer/dc/dc1000/dc1064/data/dc1064data.pdf

xvi https://www.dumbartonumc.org/our-story/our-history/b-civil-war

xvii Black Georgetown Remembers, by Lesko, Babb, and Gibbs, ISBN 978-1-64712-165-5

xviii The Old Methodist Burying Ground, a 1975 Report by Paul E. Sluby, Sr.; Genealogic Department, Church of Jesus Christ of Latter Day Saints

xix The Afro-American Bicentennial Corporation was established on 30 December 1970 and has passed out of existence.

xx https://www.washingtoninformer.com/historic-black-cemeteries-in-georgetown-recognized-by-un/

xxi A Neighborhood Guide to Washington, D.C.'s Hidden History, by Jeanne Fogle, ISBN 978-1-59629-652-7, pages 62 & 63.

xxii From the list of Washington, DC cemeteries on the Washington DC Genealogy web site

xxiii From the Oak Hill Cemetery web site: http://www.oakhillcemeterydc.org/history.html

xxiv Capital Losses – A Cultural History of Washington's Destroyed Buildings, by James M. Goode, page 195

xxv BURY ME DEEP, Burial Places Past and Present in and Nearby Washington, D.C. A Historical Review and Reference Manual by Paul S. Sluby, Sr., Page 66.

xxvi From research performed by Carlton Fletcher; available on the web at: http://gloverparkhistory.com/cemeteries/burial-grounds-of-georgetown/the-presbyterian-burial-ground-of-georgetown/

xxvii https://www.findagrave.com/memorial/14448211/stephen-bloomer-balch

xxviii

https://en.wikipedia.org/wiki/Presbyterian_Burying_Ground#Founding_the_cemetery

xxix The Presbyterian Congregation In George Town, 1780-1970. Published by the Session of the Presbyterian Congregation of George Town, Washington, D.C. 1971.

[xxx] *The Visitation- A Monastic way of life in the Church*, ISBN 978-2-7468-2091-3, 2008, page 56

[xxxi] Nation Register of Historic Places Registration Form – Georgetown Visitation Convent and Preparatory School, December 14, 1990. Page 7.

[xxxii] Ibid

[xxxiii] From the web at: https://www.amazon.com/Slave-Ship-Harvard-History-American/dp/0823239519

[xxxiv] *Black Georgetown Remembers*, by Lesko, Babb, and Gibbs, ISBN 978-1-64712-165-5

[xxxv] From the web at: https://springboardexchange.org/miacarey/

[xxxvi] Ibid

[xxxvii] From the Library of Virginia: *A guide to the Wormley Family Papers 1773 – 1991* by Renee M. Savitis

[xxxviii] https://www.gilderlehrman.org/collection/glc05111010196

[xxxix] http://www.streetsofwashington.com/2013/08/on-pennsylvania-ave-georgetowns-other.html

[xl] *The Chronicles of Georgetown, D. C. from 1751 to 1878* by Richard P. Jackson; Washington, DC; R. O. Polkinhorn, Printer; 1878

[xli] From the Thought Company website: https://www.thoughtco.com/facts-about-the-maryland-colony-103875

[xlii] From the Wikipedia entry: Georgetown (Washington, D.C.)

[xliii] Ibid

[xliv] From the National Park Service website Georgetown Historic District: http://www.nps.gov/nr/travel/wash/dc15.htm

[xlv] https://gloverparkhistory.com/population/settlement/land-tracts-2/

[xlvi] http://www.city-data.com/states/District-of-Columbia-History.html

[xlvii] *Black Georgetown Remembers*, by Lesko, Babb, and Gibbs, ISBN 978-1-64712-165-5

[xlviii] https://gloverparkhistory.com/population/settlement/land-tracts-2/

[xlix] From the DC Genealogy web site – under: Some Historic Black Churches and Cemeteries in Washington, DC.

[l] From the web site of Washington.org: http://washington.org/DC-information/washington-dc-history

[li] From the Historical Society of Washington, DC's 2022_04_07 *Experiments in Freedom: The Legacy of the DC Compensated Emancipation Act*

[lii] From a web search: www.thefullwiki.org/Georgetown,Washington,_DC
[liii] From The First Baptist Church of Georgetown, D.C. Cornerstone
[liv] From a web search: Topher Mathews, July 24, 2013
[lv] https://www.friendsofpeircemill.org/the-mills-of-rock-creek/

www.ingramcontent.com/pod-product-compliance
Lightning Source LLC
Chambersburg PA
CBHW080552170426
43195CB00016B/2765